INTERMEDIATE

KT-502-463

THIS ITEM MAY BE BORROWED FOR

ONE WEEK ONLY

INTERMEDIATE LOANS ARE IN HIGH DEMAND,
PLEASE RETURN OR RENEW

To renew, online at: http://prism.talis.com/chi-ac/
or by telephone: 01243 816089 (Bishop Otter)
01243 812099 (Bognor Regis)

2 8 MAR 2011

- 5 APR 2011

1 0 OCT 2011

NOV 2011

WITHDRAWN

WS 2286415 6

1.2011

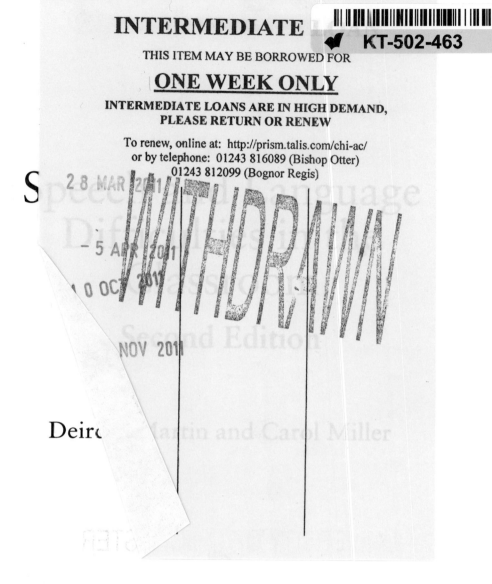

Speech and Language
Difficulties in the
Classroom

Second Edition

Deirdre Martin and Carol Miller

David Fulton Publishers

David Fulton Publishers
2 Park Square, Milton Park, Abingdon, Oxon OX14 4RN

270 Madison Avenue, New York, NY 10016

Transferred to digital printing

David Fulton Publishers is an imprint of the Taylor & Francis Group, an informa business

Copyright © Deirdre Martin and Carol Miller 2003

The right of Deirdre Martin and Carol Miller to be identified as the authors of this work has been asserted by them in accordance with the Copyright, Designs and Patents Act 1988.

British Library Cataloguing in Publication Data
A catalogue record for this book is available from the British Library.

ISBN 1 85346 845 2

All rights reserved. No part of this publication may be reproduced, stored in a retrieval system or transmitted, in any form, or by any means, electronic, mechanical, photocopying, recording or otherwise, without the prior permission of the publishers.

UNIVERSITY OF CHICHESTER

Typeset by Textype Typesetters, Cambridge

371,
91
MAR

Contents

Preface to first edition

Understanding the nature of speech and language difficulties has long been the prerogative of the few. Where there are policies encouraging integration and inclusion of children with difficulties into mainstream education, practitioners in the classroom are finding that they need to know more about the nature, assessment procedures and support strategies for a variety of special educational needs. The demand for development opportunities in this field has grown steadily and it is clear that many staff encounter pupils whose language and communication skills give rise to concern. Many of the ideas for this book have grown from our experiences in working with teachers and speech and language therapists over a number of years. Most recently, we have been involved in the professional development of practitioners to work in schools with pupils identified as having speech and language difficulties.

In this book we aim to discuss in some detail the range of speech and language difficulties which children may experience in the classroom and to offer the practitioner an educational perspective on these difficulties. We also discuss speech and language difficulties from other perspectives, namely medical, linguistic and psycholinguistic.

The strength of the medical approach to understanding speech and language difficulties lies in its attempt to identify a cause for the difficulty, although in many cases no such cause can be identified. As an alternative some practitioners look to see what the linguistic perspective offers and the application of linguistic analysis to speech and language difficulties allows us to describe in considerable detail the surface features of language. The continuing need to identify why children and young people have the difficulties they do, has led practitioners to look at language processing, and how speech and language is stored, accessed and retrieved. The most recent approach is from the the area of cognitive neuropsychology, so-called psycholinguistics, which has a substantial history of research into language processing that has recently been applied to speech and language difficulties particularly in children and young people.

Throughout the book we discuss the relationship between these approaches, pointing out their strengths in helping us to understand the nature of language difficulties as well as where they fall short of a fuller understanding. In fact, we conclude that all of these perspectives are necessary to understand the complex nature of speech and language difficulties. However, we perceive that classroom practitioners require a fourth perspective for understanding the nature and process of speech and language difficulties – an educational perspective.

We believe that the educational perspective is the one that is likely to be the most useful to those who are involved in the teaching and learning of pupils with speech and language difficulties, as well as their parents and other associated professionals. Their primary concern is to encourage and facilitate the pupils' access to the curriculum. Since language is an essential vehicle for children's learning, pupils with speech and language difficulties seem to be more challenged than most in accessing the curriculum. Furthermore, we know that many pupils with speech and language difficulties have other special educational needs as well. Most practitioners and parents feel that they need to understand these difficulties in a way that will allow them to support the pupils' curriculum learning. We think that understanding speech and language involves appreciating the patterns and processes of development in most children and, consequently, we take a developmental approach to understanding many of the difficulties.

Throughout the book we have put forward a view that an individual may have a 'difficulty' rather than a 'problem', 'disorder', 'deviance' or 'impairment', although we allude to and discuss these terms whenever they are used in the literature on this topic. We think that these terms are more in line with clinical perspectives and that the term 'difficulty' is more in line with the educational perspective. The individual's speech and language difficulty is as much a social construct as it is a processing or physical difference. In other words, the difficulty may lie with factors within the pupil but it may also lie with factors of perception and attitude of others in the pupils' social and communication contexts. Practitioners and parents must seek to address the individual's difficulties on both of these levels. They need to focus their efforts not only on supporting the pupil with language difficulties but also on influencing the pupil's peers, staff, friends and relatives.

The book opens with two chapters setting out terms, concepts and perspectives on speech and language as we intend to use them throughout the following chapters. The subsequent chapters deal with the range of speech and language difficulties which are usually recognised and identified in the classroom. We include a chapter on literacy because we agree that difficulties in reading, writing and spelling are often rooted in speech and language processing. The final two chapters focus on the professional development of practitioners, both in terms of how they work within the multidisciplinary team and also how they reflect on their practice in the classroom.

A number of our colleagues have contributed to this book. Martin Duckworth provided some of the ideas for Chapters 1 and 5; Rosemarie Hayhow contributed to Chapter 9 and Paula Halliday provided the curriculum planning framework in Chapter 10. The examples of classroom practice in Chapter 10 were selected from many excellent assignments written by teachers who have been students on the Distance Education Course in Speech and Language Difficulties at the University of Birmingham. We would particularly like to thank Gillian Fone, Carol O'Keefe and Dolina Rigg for these examples, but many others have also inspired our work. From time to time in the book we refer to feedback from teachers. We obtained this from the evaluation of the professional development courses. We are grateful to all those practitioners who were our students, for their comments.

We have written the book primarily for those practitioners who work in educational settings with pupils who have speech and language difficulties. We also hope that it will be helpful and informative to other professionals and students who work with these children and young people in settings such as clinics and training centres, in their liaison and collaboration with practitioners in the classroom. We hope, too, that it has much to offer the parents and families of these pupils in their understanding of speech and language difficulties and in their cooperation and work with the educational practitioners who are involved with their children.

Deirdre Martin and Carol Miller
Birmingham, November 1995

Preface to second edition

In the last six years since this book was first published, language and communication difficulties have received greater attention from government and policy-makers in the UK. Inclusion policies have meant that children with special learning needs should be able to access the curriculum and have opportunities to work towards aims similar to those of their peers. Their peers will also have opportunities to develop understanding and tolerance of others with different learning abilities.

The Programme of Action (Department for Education and Employment 1998a) for special education made particular mention of children with language and communication needs and the inadequacies of provision for them. As a consequence, a number of initiatives have created interest and activity related to this group of pupils. A Working Group (DfEE/DH 2000) made recommendations on the provision of speech and language therapy in education and a government-funded research project (Law et al. 2000) explored wider aspects of provision. A further project created a Joint Professional Development Framework for teachers and speech and language therapists (I CAN 2001). This has provided an impetus for the development of opportunities for practitioners to learn together, stimulated still further by the imperative of the revised Code of Practice (DfEE 2001) which says that services 'must work together'. In addition to these initiatives, English Local Educational Authorities have been supported in enhancing speech and language therapy services through grants from the Standards Fund.

There has also been more research into the nature of speech and language difficulties, notably exploring relationships between different aspects of language and related behaviour. For example, recent studies have looked at difficulties in the social use of language and autism (e.g. Bishop 2000), specifically around semantic and pragmatic difficulties. Other studies have investigated the relationship between speech and literacy (e.g. Stackhouse and Wells 1997).

Another research focus has been on the education and management of learners with speech and language needs. Some studies have extended their exploration of the nature of the difficulties into investigating intervention strategies and programmes of support (Stackhouse and Wells 2001). Others have been interested in investigating the transition of children as they move between provisions such as language units and mainstream school (Conti-Ramsden *et al.* 2001).

This second edition therefore reflects some of the changes which have been taking place. Greater emphasis on inclusion of a wider range of children in mainstream schools influences our assumption that increasing numbers of practitioners need to be informed about language and communication for learning. In the Preface to the first edition of the book, we suggested the use of the word 'difficulties' in preference to 'problems' or 'disorders' of language. Perhaps as a reflection of changing awareness of diversity in schools and the responsibility of practitioners to respond to this, we now place greater emphasis on 'needs' rather than difficulties. There is then an implication that the needs can be addressed.

The structure of the book remains the same and concludes, rightly, as before, with the experiences of teachers and speech and language therapists in practice. As well as updating references and information, we have included more on issues of assessment and intervention and on emotion and behaviour as these are now seen to be closely related to communication. In the belief that the book can only provide an introduction and that practitioners will want to know more, we have provided suggestions for further reading at the end of each chapter.

Deirdre Martin and Carol Miller
Birmingham July 2002

Chapter 1

Ways of thinking about language

Introduction

In this book we are interested in human communication. This takes many forms, for example, spoken language, of which conversation is the most common; written language; signed language. These forms comprise many elements; conversation, for example, will consist of sentences, clauses, phrases, sounds and structured interchanges between the participants. The written form has sentences, words, spelling, punctuation and a particular shape on a page. Later in the book, some of the relationships between these are discussed. Our purpose is to draw attention to how communication is such a vital part of life and to think of the implications of a difficulty in this characteristic aspect of our social relationships. Here we will briefly introduce some of the main ideas of the elements of communication and start the discussions by looking at conversation.

Conversation

Conversation is the most common form of communication which takes place every day. The variety of conversation is infinite, through the whole range of face-to-face encounters and telephone communication. We only have to think of interactions between friends and family members, discussions between doctors and patients, teachers and pupils and members of boardroom meetings to realise how much it varies in its formality and style on each unique occasion. Indeed, in any situation where people are found, there will be conversation. Yet conversation requires highly developed skills.

How does a person learn how to have a conversation? What do they do? Stop for a moment and think what you do when you have a conversation. Think of all the things that you have to do. Perhaps also, try to observe some other people in conversation to see and hear what they do. You will need to observe with your eyes and with your ears.

Firstly, it should be said that for most people, their knowledge about how to have a conversation is quite unconscious. However, this largely unconscious knowledge, built up over years, affects the content and the management of the conversation, that is, what it is about, and how the conversation takes place.

Conversation always involves more than one person. It relies on signals made by the individuals when they 'pass messages' to each other, through speech sounds and other noises, words and phrases, facial expressions, gestures and other movements of their bodies. In successful conversations, there are not too many silences, neither are there too many overlaps of speech. For the most part, people know when it is their turn in the conversation. They know this from a variety of signs: the changes in the rise and fall of the voice of their conversational partner(s); the loudness of the voice; the direction of gaze and small changes in body position and in gestures. All of these help the speakers to cooperate with each other and to take turns to speak. If you have ever tried to have a conversation with someone whose eyes never meet your own, who never seems to pause to allow you to say what you want to say, or who does not pick up what you have said, you will know how difficult conversation can be. On the other hand, in most conversations, it would be unusual if the people spoke perfectly in turn and always waited for their partner to finish what they were saying. Perhaps more surprisingly, if the conversation was written down, or transcribed, exactly as it had been said, it would be unusual to find that the speakers had spoken in what might be described as 'complete sentences'.

The linguist's view

Linguistics, the science of language, is concerned with classifying and analysing the features of language, how it is used and how it is structured. Linguists are interested in the components or levels of language. To look at language and communication in some detail, it can be broken down into its components and it becomes necessary to have some words to talk about what we are describing. First, two of the most commonly used terms used to discuss human communication are 'speech' and 'language'. They are often used interchangeably although it is quite possible and indeed, common, to have language without speech, as in sign languages. Speech is only one form of language. It is a way of using the sounds of the human voice to communicate. We can also use writing, or signs. Speech is the audible (spoken) form of language.

Components of language

For the purposes of discussion, in this book we will often refer separately to the components of spoken language. This might lead you to believe that speech sounds, grammar and meaning are unrelated to each other. A moment's reflection about the way in which you use language at an interview, compared with, for example, when you are talking informally to a good friend, will probably alert you to the effect that the context and purpose of communication has on pronunciation and choice of words. The academic study of language is a very large field so that the separation of its components is probably inevitable. However, the sound, grammar and meaning levels operate together in our *use* of language. The components are therefore integrated and interdependent. Nevertheless, in order to examine the main components a little more carefully, we will consider them separately. We will consider the sounds, grammar and meaning.

The sounds of language

When referring to the sound components of a language, linguists usually distinguish between phonetics and phonology.

Phonology
The study of the capacity of speech sounds to change the meaning in language is known as phonology. Look at the list of words below and notice how the change of the vowel sound alone changes a word's meaning:

beat, bit, bait, bet, bat, bought, boat, boot, butt, bite, bout, Bert.
(Adapted from Ladefoged 1982: 70)

If you read the list aloud, you will hear the vowels used in your particular way of pronouncing English, that is, your accent or regional variation. For interest, ask other people, including if possible, some foreign speakers, to read the list and notice the differences in the way they speak. Phonology examines the system or patterns of sounds used in language.

An everyday example of the exploitation of phonology can be found in the cartoon feature in a national newspaper, known as 'Lost Consonants'. It draws its humour from the change in meaning which one consonant can make to a sentence. In many cases, this loss of a consonant means the loss of a sound and, as a consequence, a change in meaning. For example:

'He was very fond of a tory at bedtime'
'He finally found work as a long distance lorry drier'
'To deter illegal parking, police introduced wheel lamps'.

(Rawle 1992)

Phonetics

It is important to remember that in English, the alphabet does not correspond to the sounds of the language and there are certainly more vowel sounds than 'a', 'e' 'i' 'o' and 'u'. Sounds of speech do not always correspond to the letters of the alphabet or the way in which a word is spelled.

In order to write down sounds of a language and to avoid the complex spelling rules found in languages like English, the International Phonetic Alphabet (IPA) is used. This has a one-to-one correspondence between symbol and sound. For example, in English the last sounds in the words *kiss* and *palace* are written quite differently but would be written /s/ and /s/ phonetically; the sound at the beginning of *fun* and at the beginning and the end of *photograph* would also have the same phonetic symbol. Conversely, the words *circus* and *comb* begin with the same letter but would have to be written with a different phonetic symbol to convey the different initial sounds. The vowels in the words *he*, *beat*, *sheet* and *key* may sound the same but they are written differently. Analysis at the phonetic level considers the way in which sounds are made, how they differ and how they are similar.

Prosody

A final and important aspect of speech pronunciation is known as prosody. That is the stress, intonation and voice quality used in spoken communication. In English, intonation and stress can change the meaning of an utterance without changing the words. Say each of the following first as a statement and then as a question:

You've been working
The shop was closed
You think he's good-looking

Next, say the first sentence as though you feel sorry for the person you are talking to. Say the second as though you are angry. Say the third as though you don't believe 'he' is good-looking.

For all of the above activities it would be useful to tape-record yourself and listen to the result.

You can see that the variations in the rises and falls of your voice, the loudness of your voice, the speed of your speech and the emphasis you put on words or parts of words makes quite a difference to the meaning of what you are saying. Note that at no time did you change the words or the order in which you used them.

Grammar

The next way in which we may describe language is by considering the grammar or the rules by which the words and parts of words are put together. These rules will determine the ordering of words, so for example *I saw her* is acceptable in English but *I her saw* is not. The way in which words are structured to convey specific meaning is also governed by rules: *The boy kick the ball* is unacceptable but *The boy kicked the ball* or *The boy kicks the ball* is acceptable depending on the meaning the speaker wishes to convey.

Consider the following examples and try to say exactly where a rule is broken:

1. I playing football yesterday
2. I bought a pair of sock

In example 1, the ending *-ing* conveys the present tense of the verb *play* and so is incompatible with the word *yesterday* which suggests the past tense. In order to be acceptable the sentence should be *I played football yesterday*.

In the second example, the word *pair* indicates that the plural form of the word *sock* is required so that an acceptable sentence would be *I bought a pair of socks*.

The small parts of words which change their meaning, from singular to plural or from one tense to another, are known as **morphemes** and the study of this aspect of language is known as **morphology**. The ordering of words and parts of words is governed by the rules of **syntax**. Morphology and syntax make up the grammar of a language.

Meaning

Next, the choice of words and the function they perform will be an important aspect of the meaning of language. In the study of the meaning of language, **semantics** is the term used.

Much of the understanding of a word's meaning comes from our knowledge of the linguistic and the social context in which it is used. Briefly, the linguistic context is the other words and linguistic elements which surround the word in question. In English, many words have the same written form but different meanings. Just consider different meanings of the word *swallow*; *table*; *page*. Further, words which are written differently can have the same pronunciation, for example, *sole* and *soul*; *write* and *right*.

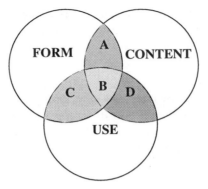

Figure 1.1 The intersection of content, form, and use in language (Bloom and Lahey, 1978)

Unless you hear or read these words in the context of connected speech or written language you will not understand their specific meaning. The social context, that is, who is speaking and where they are, will be important factors in determining the choice of words used. This will influence the shared meaning, which is essential when considering how people understand each other.

Content, form and use

Our discussions above have focused on the complex and overlapping components or levels of human communication. In order to think about the very complicated system more simply, we can think of these components under three headings: the *meaning* or *content* of the communication, the *structure* or *form* and the *function* of the communication. Each aspect is essential for communication to be effective. Two American researchers, Lois Bloom and Margaret Lahey, have presented these ideas clearly by means of three overlapping circles (a Venn diagram) Figure 1.1.

   Content refers to the topics and ideas that are put together or 'encoded' in messages. It reflects what we know about people, things, actions. The content of our communications shows that we are able to make relationships between ideas, to consider how things are similar, different and associated with each other. The content represents and allows access to concepts which are stored in our memory.

   Form is the way in which meaning is represented. This may be through speech, signs, writing or another systematic form. It consists of an inventory of units, for example, sounds, marks on a page or movements, and the system of rules for their combination. In the context of spoken language these would be referred to as phonology, morphology and syntax.

Use has to be considered from two points of view: use or function, and context. Function refers to the goals of language, the reasons why people speak. Context refers to how individuals understand and choose among alternative forms for reaching the same or different goals. In linguistic terms, the functional level of language is known as pragmatics.

One of the strengths of Bloom and Lahey's model is that it shows how aspects of language interconnect and yet can be identified separately. It shows how it is possible to explain that the language difficulties of an individual might arise from difficulties predominantly in one area or across more than one of these areas. However, the model cannot show that within each of these areas there are different theoretical frameworks which can explain and predict the functioning of that aspect of language. Further, within an area such as Form, the levels of language, syntax and phonology are studied in different ways. This is also the case for Content and Use. We will consider these later.

Language development in children

The brief outline of the features of language demonstrates the complexity of human communication, yet most children are skilled communicators by the time they go to school. By the age of five, the majority of children have mastered many of the rules of grammar, have a wide vocabulary and can make themselves understood to a range of people in a variety of situations. Their language development is not complete; indeed, communication skills continue to develop throughout life, but the main features are in place. In this book, we can only give a broad account of how children learn to communicate. It is important that practitioners who are concerned about children's language should be clear about patterns of development and about the main influences on this development. Further reading can be found in the list at the end of the chapter.

What is it then, that a child has to develop to become an effective communicator? What has to be available and what does the child have to do? It is helpful to consider these questions because, if we can identify what usually happens, then we may begin to understand why some children experience difficulties in learning to communicate. First, what does the child have to learn?

We noted above that conversation can only take place when there are at least two people. A child usually becomes aware of this very early in life through the contact with attentive adults. Adults frequently talk to young babies as though they understood every word and it is thought that these early contacts enable the child to 'tune in' to the sight and sound of people. There is evidence that in the first few weeks of life babies start to prefer the sound of familiar human voices over other, non-human sounds and they quickly learn to recognise familiar faces (Bower 1980). The sounds made by infants are often stimuli for 'conversations' with adults. An adult will often pick up and imitate a baby's gurgles and coos and begin the early turn-taking which is later an important element of conversation (Richards 1974). It seems as though the foundations for communication are laid very early.

It can be very difficult to determine the exact time when a child uses its first real word, indeed, in some ways, the first word often seems to be in the mind (or the ear) of the adult. For example, a parent may be delighted that their child says *da* and may interpret this as *dad* or *daddy*. They may go on to interpret this utterance further, according to the time and place in which it was said. For example, if the child said *da* as they heard someone come through the door, an adult may respond with *Ah, here's daddy*. However, if the child was playing on the floor and picked up an article, saying *da*, the response might be *Oh, you've found daddy's sock*. The adult uses information about what is going on at the time to decide what the child might mean. They impose the meaning of a whole sentence on the child's utterance of a single syllable. What seems to be important is that the adult gives a response to the child and says something relevant to the situation in return. The child begins to learn that their utterances will meet with responses in different circumstances. Of course, the clarity of children's utterances in the early stages is affected by their limited command of sounds and they often produce combinations of sounds which are in some way similar to adult words rather than exact replications.

The situation is similar when children begin to use more than single syllables. They may point and, with rising intonation say *ada* which the attentive adult interprets as *What's that?* and gives an appropriate reply. The child's utterance therefore, carries real meaning, is quite different from that of an adult, yet it can be understood because of its context. As we suggested earlier, social context, or the situation in which communication takes place, is an extremely important consideration and will continue to be so throughout life. It is impossible to make judgements about a child's attempts to communicate without taking into account the context in which they are used.

Single syllable utterances which resemble adult words and phrases will be limited in their use. They are really only functional if very familiar people are present who are paying great attention. As the child's need to communicate with a wider group of people in a variety of situations develops, the need for clearer speech and more complex utterances is evident. We can say that the child begins to use grammar when they combine syllables and words to produce meaningful utterances. In the early stages, these utterances are still very much bound to contexts. A child coming into the room, holding a cup and saying *mummy cup* may mean, *This is mummy's cup, Look mummy, this is my cup* or even *Mummy give me a drink in this cup*. Only the situation and the occurrences around it will allow an appropriate interpretation.

A further stage of development seems to provide us with good evidence that children are beginning to learn grammatical rules. Parents and teachers are very familiar with 'errors' which children make such as *I drinked it all up; mouses*. However, these odd examples suggest that a child knows that on many occasions, adding '-ed' to a verb will give it a past tense meaning; adding 's' to a word will make it a plural. The problem is, there are some words to which these rules do not apply, but until a child knows that the past tense of *drink* is *drank* and the plural of *mouse* is *mice* they overgeneralise and use the rules that they already know. Such examples are important evidence that a child's language is developing. They tell us, for example, that the child has a concept of past tense and of plurality. They are evidence that the child can apply what they have learned in other situations to new contexts and can be creative with what they already know.

Possible explanations

After looking at some of the observable features of children's early language development, we need to stop to consider some of the explanations which have been put forward for how and why this all happens.

Two of the most important ideas about the nature of language and language development to emerge in the latter part of the twentieth century came from two North Americans, Skinner and Chomsky. Skinner was a psychologist who proposed a powerful hypothesis for explaining and predicting how learning takes place. It has become known as the Stimulus-Response-Reward pattern or, because it focuses on human behaviour changes, *behaviourism*. Skinner (1957) proposed that through this model all learning took place, including language learning. For example, he argued that when infants heard a sound or a word (Stimulus) they would try to imitate it (Response) and then their efforts would be praised by the adult (Reward). In this way, through Stimulus-Response-Reward patterning the child would acquire a vocabulary and grammatical structures. Skinner proposed imitation and repetition as key features in language learning.

In 1959, Noam Chomsky, a linguist and mathematician, challenged this theory and argued that it was profoundly flawed and seriously misunderstood the nature of language. Chomsky argued that language was not learned in the same way as other areas of knowledge and thus the Stimulus-Response-Reward pattern was not applicable to language. He suggested that the human brain has a template to acquire language. He called this the language acquisition device (LAD), which is capable of generating language and linguistic structures. He also argued that language, in particular grammar, was not learned word by word. Language is learned as a system and not as isolated parts, as we saw in our section above on language development in children.

In contrast to these theories, there have been two influential approaches by European psychologists, Piaget and Vygotsky, who have taken a social-cognitive view. Many practitioners in education are more familiar with these ideas.

Piaget did not agree with Chomsky's claim that language and in particular grammar, developed autonomously. Piaget argued that language, including grammar, developed within the framework of more general cognitive development. Although language emerged later than other cognitive functions and may well be dependent on them it was not exceptionally different from general cognitive development. Language development was about the child coming to know and understand the elements, the structures and the function of language just as the child would learn about other patterns and relationships such as quantity and probability. Finally, Piaget saw the child as a 'little scientist', exploring the world, solving problems and learning language alone. A useful summary of Piaget's theories is given by Donaldson (1978), whose research reinterpreted some of Piaget's work.

The idea of a child operating in isolation was strongly challenged by the Russian psychologist, Vygotsky (1962), who emphasised the importance of other people for children's learning. He saw language as a tool both for sharing experiences with others and for developing and organising thinking. Although children do explore and learn as they discover the world, Vygotsky suggested that this is influenced in a major way by adults and others who are more competent than the child. Much of children's learning takes place in conjunction with others who support and develop the child's skills further.

Bruner (1986) called this support 'scaffolding'. It is not difficult to imagine how this applies to the development of language, which is essentially social and is developed in interactions with others. Bruner describes how the games and activities played by parents with infants provide experiences which advance the child's knowledge and understanding. As a child responds to parents' questions and comments, such as *What's that?* or *Look at that*, the parent then moves on, expecting new and different responses and 'remains forever on the growing edge of the child's competence' (p.77). According to Vygotsky, these interactions influence thinking and conceptualisation, which are clearly related to the development of language. The essential factor is the nurturing by others of a child who is ready to learn.

Among the most recent explorations of language development in children are those which emphasise the cognitive aspects of language processing. This has been done by combining ideas from the fields of psychology, linguistics and neurology. The approach is sometimes called the developmental cognitive neurolinguistic or psycholinguistic framework.

The cognitive neurolinguistic framework is based on four elements: the way that the brain is organised for language, the cognitive or neuronal architecture; the storage of information, mental representations; the processing of tasks; the output (Dockrell and McShane 1993). The most important part of the cognitive architecture is the working memory which stores auditory and visual information to be used immediately, or the information may be stored permanently in the long-term memory. For example, information about the speech sound sequence of a word would be stored as a phonological mental representation. Processing, which is mainly unconscious and automatic, permits information to be manipulated and understood. With new and unfamiliar material children seem to develop conscious processing strategies such as thinking about how to pronounce a word or how to form a sentence. It is suggested that there may be mental representations for organising output which seem to be similar to Piaget's schemata. In language, the production of speech is thought to rely on these output representations which organise the programming of motor speech acts.

To conclude this section on possible explanations, it seems that there are useful parts in all of the theories although no single explanation is completely satisfactory. For example, Chomsky's idea that human beings are innately predisposed to learn language is now widely accepted, as we see, for example, in the idea of cognitive architecture for language. Although Skinner's explanation of child language development is largely unsupported, some children can be taught communiation and language skills by using a behaviourist approach. This may be exploited in some teaching and intervention which is based on behaviourist learning methods. Piaget's explanation has led us to take account of children's cognitive development in assisting their language development and Vygotsky's view has increasingly led us to perceive the child as an active social learner of language with other people as essential participants. We therefore can consider children to have the cognitive predisposition to learn language which is developed by interaction with other people.

Processes and prerequisites

In order to understand more about a child's language development, it is helpful to look not only at what the child is learning but at how this is happening. We need to understand the processes and the prerequisites which enable a child to make the most of the experiences which are available.

To take advantage of the language of other people, a child needs to be able to receive it, to store it and then to produce it in some form. The majority of infants will be exposed to spoken language. Hearing or the auditory senses will therefore be important if the child is to receive the spoken messages and there will also be a visual element as the child learns about facial expressions and body movements. If the child is exposed to other forms of language, for example, a signed language, then the language will be visually received. Most children quickly learn to combine the two sensory mechanisms as they begin to look towards a person speaking and to turn to see where a noise has originated. Auditory and visual skills develop in conjunction with muscle control and movement. Head control, sitting and standing will influence what the child can see and hear. One essential therefore, for the receipt of language, is a working sensory system, often hearing, sometimes vision, but usually a combination of these, together with the development of movement.

Making use of the senses is called perception and this depends on experience and learning. We said earlier that even tiny infants prefer human voices to other sounds. They also pay more attention to human faces than to other shapes and visual stimuli. Presumably this is because humans are more interesting to them at this stage than other sights and sounds. We all pay attention to things we are interested in and attention is an important aspect of learning to communicate or indeed, learning to do anything. By paying attention, a child picks out a particular sound or set of sounds from other noises which may be going on in the background. It may be no coincidence that often adults are very close to young children when they speak to them. This may help the child to pay attention and to listen more easily.

Auditory perception, or listening, is important if a child is to learn the different sounds of speech, the rhythm of speech and the way words are put together. If you are familiar with young babies, you may have noticed that even at the age of a few weeks, their vocalisations are very tuneful and even begin to sound like the patterns in adult speech. This is evidence that the child is using its hearing very well and children who cannot hear may often be distinguished by the flat tone of their voices. Similarly, babies will use their visual skills to see how people move their mouths and their bodies when they communicate. If you are face to face with a baby of a few months old, you can play a game of opening and closing your mouth and see that often the baby will copy you. They watch very intently.

Memory also plays a part in all of this. A child will need to remember things heard or things seen so that they can recall them for future use. We all do this. When we go into situations, we need to know whether things are familiar or new. We need to draw from our memory information about what to do and what to say. Children begin to lay down information in their memories right from the beginning.

A child needs to be able to draw on memory and to use it in a huge variety of ways to suit new situations. It seems as though in the beginning children use their information in a very general way. Any furry object may be a *dog* (or just a *do*). With development and experience though, this will be refined and the child will learn to distinguish between a wide range of furry objects, animate and inanimate, and to give them appropriate names – *dog, cat, horse*. As their physical or motor control develops, they begin to say the names more clearly and gradually learn to say *dog* instead of *gog* and *cat* instead of *tat*.

The key features of early language development outlined above suggest that some very complex processes occur in young children. A biologist called Lenneberg (1967) claimed that language developed through the biological maturation of physical and perceptual processes. He suggested that the optimum period for acquiring language is between birth and puberty. After about 12 years of age, he claimed, the brain's language acquisition facilities diminish. Children who suffer brain trauma and language loss when young are more likely to recover their language fully than those who suffer language loss after brain trauma in adolescence and adulthood.

When language development proceeds well, children are usually fairly skilled communicators by the time they start school. If you think back to the model of language presented by Lois Bloom and Margaret Lahey in Figure 1.1 above, you will see that children are gradually developing the components, content, form and use in their language. As they learn to interact with a wider variety of people in a range of situations, their understanding and expression through language extends. The increasing clarity of their speech which results as they develop their articulation of sounds changes the form of their language and by using more complex structures they can convey increasingly sophisticated meanings, or content.

From the end of the first year, until the child is ten years of age or more, we can observe developments in each of these areas. If you look back to Figure 1.1, you will be able to see that as the child becomes ever more competent in each of the three areas, part D of the diagram represents the way in which each of the areas is integrated with the others to represent effective communication.

All of this suggests to us that the development of language and speech depends on a very critical interaction between what goes on around them and what is happening within a child. The child must be able to hear or see, to pay attention and remember and to make distinctions between things heard and seen. Opportunities to communicate must be provided. They must have something interesting to see and to listen to and they must have around them people who are interested and responsive. They must be able to use this information, to put it together in various combinations in order to produce 'messages'. By this we mean that they must be able to put words together in ways that other people can understand. They must have the physical strength and coordination to do this. If we are faced with a child who does not seem to be communicating as well as we would hope, we need to consider whether all of these aspects are adequate. This may help to explain why some children can be said to have speech or language difficulties. It may also suggest some of the things we might do to help.

Language in education

After taking this broad look at language and language development we need to see how it links with language in school and how it is viewed in educational contexts. It is usually assumed that children will have developed certain language skills when they begin school. Indeed, children whose language skills do not match up with the demands of the classroom may be among those considered to have speech or language difficulties. Language is obviously important in education as it is the main tool for teaching and learning in schools. Ideas in all areas of the curriculum and in all aspects of school life are conveyed through spoken and written language.

School curriculum documents will usually clarify what is expected of pupils and it is important to think about these demands. In England, the English curriculum, which is, in practice, the curricular definition of a language curriculum, is divided into speaking and listening; reading; writing (Department for Education and Employment and Qualifications and Curriculum Authority 1999). In Scotland, 'the development of skill in talking' is identified as a major aim of teaching in the English language area (Jefferies and Dolan 1994). With minor modifications, language in most school contexts can be considered in these terms. The way that speaking and listening are described suggests that children in school will use their skills of conversation, which we discussed above. In the primary school, effective speaking and listening would mean that a child could: 'speak clearly, thinking about the needs of their listeners' (Department for Education and Employment and Qualifications and Curriculum Authority 1999).

In order to achieve this, children would need to develop a range of skills. Most pupils would be developing their fluency and confidence in using spoken language, although it is accepted that some children might use an alternative to speech, perhaps signs or symbols. They would express themselves with increasing clarity and show a developing understanding of others. Their ability to communicate would be apparent in a variety of situations and with different people.

These expressions of the components of a language curriculum are consistent with the levels of language referred to earlier. The development of an ability to adapt to a variety of speaking situations, to speak with increasing clarity and to understand others is about paying attention, listening, using more complex grammar and meaning and using a wide range of sounds in the expression of clear speech. It is also about the management of conversation.

In school, of course, the language curriculum also has a written component and it is accepted that the use of written language develops from the skills of speaking and listening (Stackhouse 1989). There has been increasing emphasis on literacy skills in recent years to the extent that, in England a National Literacy Strategy was introduced, with a Framework for Teaching (Department for Education and Employment 1998b). This acknowledges that, 'Literacy unites the important skills of reading and writing' (DfEE 1998a: 3).

The skills of literacy at each level are described in terms of word, sentence and text, focusing on phonics, spelling and vocabulary, grammar and punctuation and comprehension and composition. Pupils are expected to be made aware of the sounds of spoken language in order to develop phonological awareness. They should also be taught to use various approaches to word recognition and to use their understanding of grammatical structure and the meaning of the text as a whole to make sense of what they read. (Department for Education and Employment and Qualifications and Curriculum Authority 1999).

There are assumptions here about children's understanding and use of language. Children's ability to read will be characterised, for example, by awareness of the patterns of sounds and the ways symbols correspond to those sounds. They will use syntactic and contextual clues to check and confirm meaning.

For most children it would be difficult to read accurately and fluently if they could not already speak 'accurately and fluently'. Awareness of sounds and syntactic clues would be difficult if the child did not already have these as components of their own language. Understanding of literature and texts assumes that a child already understands language. In a similar way, the writing component of the curriculum suggests skills which would be impossible for a child with poorly developed language. 'Simple spelling conventions', 'increasing vocabulary' and 'a growing ability to construct and convey ideas' are required. There is an increasing body of research which suggests strong links between children's spoken language and their ability to learn to read and write. Awareness of sounds and rhymes, as developed through nursery rhymes and simple songs, has been found to help children in learning to make sense of the rules of written language (Goswami and Bryant 1990). It is necessary for practitioners who work in classrooms with young children to know something about the components of language. They are in a position to make detailed observations of what children understand, what children say and how they say it in a variety of contexts. They should also be able to keep a record of how a child's spoken and written language is developing. Through such activities some children may be identified who cannot use language adequately for learning in school.

Conclusion

In this chapter we have very briefly discussed the nature and characteristics of communication and language. We have also looked at the main ideas on how young children acquire language. In one chapter it is impossible to provide great detail. The study of language and language development is wide and there are many sources of further information. We hope that this chapter has provided some of the main terms used for the description of language and that the reader is aware of the complexities of language. In the next chapter, we look more specifically at language which gives cause for concern and consider some of the possible reasons why language may fail to develop.

Further reading

Bee, H. (2000) *The Developing Child.* (9th edn). London: Allyn and Bacon.

Crystal, D. (1997) *The Cambridge Encyclopedia of Language.* (2nd edn). Cambridge: Cambridge University Press.

Mercer, N. (2000) *Words and Minds: How We Use Language to Think Together.* London: Routledge.

Whitehead, M.R. (2002) *Language and literacy in the early years.* (2nd edn). London: Paul Chapman.

Chapter 2

Speech and language difficulties: an overview

Introduction

The last chapter provided some of the theoretical perspectives on language and language development. In this chapter we develop aspects of these themes to consider the nature of speech and language difficulties in children. We consider the different ways in which language difficulties can be viewed and some of the reasons why there are differing perspectives.

The study of speech and language difficulties is relatively young and there have been considerable developments in the field since the 1970s. The basis of the study has broadened and includes views from a wide range of related disciplines, for example, psychology, linguistics, education, anatomy and physiology and medicine. Crystal and Varley (1998) note that there have been considerable advances in investigative techniques and analytic procedures which have produced 'enormous amounts of fresh data' and there is an increasing 'awareness of the limitations of traditional categories, nomenclature and practices'. There is also a particular difficulty of inconsistent use of terms relating to language by people who try to work together. Thus, as in many areas of discussion in education, particularly in special education, the terminology in the field of speech and language difficulties in children is complex and continues to change. It may appear confused and often to be conflicting because of specific biases of professional groups and the consequent differences between their views.

First, when is a 'difficulty' a 'problem'? There are many varieties of a spoken language. A wide range of ways of talking is possible and acceptable. It is important to be clear about what is a normal variation and what really is a problem. It is also essential to consider the views of those involved with a child who is thought to have a problem. Do they think there is a problem? We know that parents can take their child to the doctor because they are worried about their speech, only to be told, 'don't worry, they'll grow out of it'. In these cases the doctor seems to have a different view of a problem from a parent. This will be very important when we come to the management of difficulties as then it will be essential to look at how an individual child fits into the context of a particular family or school system.

Children vary widely in their rates and patterns of language acquisition and there are differences in attitudes to spoken language. In Britain, opinions about accents and dialects have been, and sometimes still are, associated with beliefs about intelligence and social class (Giles and Powesland 1978). Acceptability of language varies. Different values are attached to the use of verbal interaction. Consider your own views of the way people talk. Why do you like listening to some people and not to others? People who have teenage children are sometimes heard telling them to 'talk properly'. Is it because of the way they pronounce words; because their voices are too loud or too quiet or because they never seem to pause for breath? Does this mean they have a speech or language difficulty? Is it a problem? For whom? Practitioners in education need to be aware of the wide variations in use of language and the flexibility of use available to most people. We can usually understand people with a different accent from our own and we often adapt the way that we talk to meet the needs of the situation we are in. However, the children we are concerned with in this book do not seem to have this choice. Their access to language is inhibited for a variety of reasons.

How many children are there?

The wide range of views about language and language difficulties means that it is difficult to know exactly how many children experience special needs in learning speech and language. Surveys use different definitions and categorise problems in a variety of ways. Language changes as children grow and develop so that figures will be different for different age groups. It is important, however, to have some reasonable estimate of numbers of children we can expect. The planning of educational, social and health services relies heavily on estimated numbers of individuals with different needs. For example, how many pupils with language learning needs could the teacher of a reception class expect? How many children might be considered to need speech and language therapy?

Some studies group together children who seem to have difficulties specifically in communication with those whose speech or language needs are associated with other developmental difficulties such as physical disability, learning difficulties, hearing problems or autism. To add further to the problem, different studies use different methods of assessment and different 'cut-off' points will be used to determine when there is considered to be a speech or language difficulty.

It has been suggested that perhaps one in ten children, across the age groups, have language and communication learning needs (Law *et al.* 2000). As we might expect, more difficulties are observed in younger children and the figures become less as age increases. However, where language difficulties persist, in older children, they are likely to be more severe. Further, the studies generally show that boys are more likely to be identified than girls, perhaps twice as many, although there has so far been no satisfactory explanation for this. Although figures vary somewhat, this suggests that many staff, particularly in primary schools, can expect to meet pupils whose communication skills present difficulties.

Terminology

The classification of speech and language difficulties has traditionally fallen into two general forms: terms which give a name to a problem and those which indicate a cause or underlying problem. Many of the terms used to name speech and language problems have the medical prefix 'dys', which means a lack of function or ability. We thus find the terms, dysphasia, dyspraxia, dysarthria and dyslexia, meaning various forms of spoken and written language difficulty. One of the problems with these terms is that each will be interpreted in various ways by different people. Each term will cover a wide range of signs and features and, most importantly, will give little suggestion of strategies which may help to alleviate the problem.

The second type of classification of speech and language difficulties indicates what is assumed to be the main contributor to the problem, so that we find, for example, 'hearing impairment', 'cleft palate', 'cerebral palsy'. We can criticise this in a similar way because it gives little indication of the nature of the speech or language difficulty. For example, to know that a child has 'cleft palate speech' seems to imply that it will be the same for all children. This is not the case and such a term may be unhelpful. Similarly, children with hearing impairment may or may not have difficulties with spoken language. It is important to appreciate that giving a name to a problem does not make it easier to understand. It may lead us to make unfounded assumptions. What is more, categorising problems in this way seems to emphasise that the problem is within the individual. There is no indication of need, or of how other people may contribute to the problem.

Traditionally, communication problems have been categorised as problems of speech, language, voice, fluency. In this book, we are mainly concerned with the needs which arise as a result of difficulties in learning 'speech' and 'language' but in fact, there are few clear-cut examples. Disfluency, in which the features of sentence stress, rhythm and intonation can be disrupted may, in some cases be related to difficulties of language. For example, perhaps the child has difficulties in thinking of the right word to say or in putting words together. This results in communication which is hesitant, excessively slow or repetitive. It may be called stuttering or stammering, the terms are synonymous. In some cases, in certain situations a child may develop a fear of speaking which may lead them to substitute a different word. Problems of voice, in which the voice is persistently hoarse or even absent, are rare in children but they may lead to, or arise from, problems of social interaction. Because the various components of language are so interdependent, a feature of one aspect will affect and be affected by others.

There is a very unclear distinction between a speech difficulty and a language difficulty and many people probably use the terms interchangeably. Strictly, a speech difficulty would mean that a person had difficulty making sounds, but unclear speech may be linked with other difficulties. It may be unclear because the person cannot think of the right words to say, or they may not be able to put words or sounds in the right order. A language difficulty can occur at any of the levels of language, at the level of sounds and grammatical structure, at the level of meaning and in the way language is used for social purposes. We can think of speech as what goes on 'on the surface' but we need to probe a little further to find out exactly where the difficulty lies.

Delay, disorder, impairment . . .?

The literature often draws a distinction between 'delay' and 'disorder' when discussing children's language. Delay is said to be language similar to that which would be expected from a younger child and disorder is considered to be somehow quantitatively and qualitatively different from it. The distinction, however, is rarely so clear. Some children will use sounds, structures or words which would be expected from a much younger child. As they develop, their spoken language catches up and it is possible to say, in retrospect, that their language was 'delayed'. For other children, observation over time does not show this type of development and their difficulties may be longer lasting. Their language difficulty seems to be out of proportion with other aspects of their development, which are progressing quite well. This type of more persistent language difficulty may be called a 'language disorder' or sometimes, a 'specific' language difficulty.

The research literature usually distinguishes between children whose language difficulty seems to be associated with other developmental difficulties, for example, hearing impairment, physical disability or other learning problems, and those whose language problem seems to be 'specific' (Adams *et al.* 1997). It is not usually possible to describe the exact nature of a child's needs at one meeting and it would be very rare to be able to predict the outcomes. It is usually only by following a child's development over time that the nature of the difficulties can be described.

The debate continues about when a language delay becomes a disorder. The terms are used commonly, imprecisely and often interchangeably. You should also be aware that people use the terms language disability and 'language impairment' without too much consideration of the context of these terms. All of the terms will be relative to particular settings and social groups. People may experience an inability to speak in certain settings but not in others; for example, a child who manages quite well at home with familiar people may be limited by the demands of the school curriculum. Increasingly the term 'impairment' has been adopted but there is still an implication that the problem lies within the child and there is no indication of the responsibility of others for reducing the problem. We hope that you will become more conscious of the inadequacy of the terms and become concerned to have accurate descriptions of what a child can and cannot do with their language in particular circumstances. You will then, we hope, start to ask people, 'what do you mean?' when they tell you that a child has a language disorder or impairment or disability. You will also note who is making the assertion. Is it the child's parent, the teacher, a doctor, a speech and language therapist? Do they all agree? For all of the reasons above, it is probably more useful to talk about 'needs'. If we can identify the child's learning needs in aspects of communication and interaction, then we can try to address those needs and minimise the difficulties. An emphasis on needs places responsibility on those around the child to take action.

Patterns of development

The idea of 'patterns' of language development is helpful when we are trying to decide whether a child has particular difficulties. All children develop at different rates but the stages of development are more predictable. In some ways, language resembles other developmental skills. With minor variations, children stand before they can walk and walk before they can run. Some children crawl and others shuffle on their bottoms. When parents are worried by 'shuffling' they can be reassured that walking will follow shortly because there is plenty of evidence from thousands of children that these are predictable stages (Robson 1984). In a similar way, speech and language development follows certain patterns, with some variations and at different rates. In order to be aware of the patterns, it is important to note features of the child's language over time, say for a period of a few months. It is also important to be clear about what most other children would be able to do at the same age and stage of development, if they have had similar experiences and opportunities. By doing this, we can see if the development is going along slowly, or quickly compared with our expectations. In some cases, development may be patchy and the child may show odd areas of good ability but difficulties in others. There may be some children whose development stands still or regresses. This sometimes happens, for example, if they receive a head injury or have a progressive disease. This information will be set against what we know about the early stages of a child's communication development. Did it start early, at about the expected time, or were they late to start communicating?

A few children start to talk early and development of speech and language is fast. For the majority of children the onset and rate of speech and language development compares with most others. There should be no concerns about any of these children. Others may be late starting to talk but then their speech and language development may accelerate and they will have no later difficulties. Although there were early concerns about them, there is no longer any need for worry. Children whose late development does not accelerate will present with a speech and language delay and this may be associated with other learning difficulties. Similarly, the child whose speech and language shows patchy development, whose development stops or regresses, will probably need further attention and investigation.

An educational perspective

Whenever there is concern about any aspect of a child's development, we need some ways to explain and understand what is happening. A systematic and questioning approach is required which draws on information from a range of sources.

We have said a number of times that it is important to describe in detail what we see and hear when a child's communication skills do not meet the demands we make of them. We need to describe what the child does, what other people are doing and where it is all taking place. This approach to understanding the difficulties is about considering behaviour in context.

We must consider not a child with a problem but a child with needs. In classrooms, no one works in isolation. Children's responses must always be considered in terms of other people's behaviour and what is expected. In school, we have to take account, not only of how a child communicates, but of how other people use language. This means looking carefully at the language that is used and demanded for the curriculum and other classroom activities. Before deciding that a child has a speech or a language 'difficulty' we need to consider whether the language used by teachers and other adults is appropriate and what the adults are expecting of the child. We all mishear things at times, especially if the meaning is unclear. As illustrations of this, we can probably all think of amusing examples, which do not usually amount to 'problems'.

At Easter, a young child came home from school singing 'Prices risen', a misperception of 'Christ is risen'.

Although fictional, the following example, or something similar, has probably been repeated numerous times in reality:

> The News was boring but sometimes I watched it properly, all of it. I thought that the Americans were fighting gorillas in Vietnam; that was what it sounded like. But it didn't make any kind of sense. The Israelis were always fighting the Arabs and the Americans were fighting the gorillas. It was nice that the gorillas had a country of their own, not like the zoo. . .
>
> (Doyle 1993: 227)

Neither of the examples above should suggest that a child has a language problem or difficulty but they may have a particular need to listen more carefully or to have things explained to them more slowly than other children. They are examples of what happens many times a day in classrooms when children misinterpret what adults say to them and adults do not check whether they have been understood. The curriculum can be full of hazards if new vocabulary and concepts are introduced without careful checking that everyone understands each new word and idea. If the language of the teacher and the language of the curriculum have been taken into account, there may be children who still seem to have greater difficulty than most of the others in their group. It may then be necessary to look in more detail at that child and at the circumstances surrounding their attempts to communicate. The following activity may be helpful.

Examining language

Think of a child whose speech is somehow 'different' from others.

- What is it that concerns you?
- What can the child do or not do compared with other children?
- What do others, including yourself, do when communicating with the child?

You should try to describe exactly what it is that concerns you. Is it that people cannot understand what the child says? – or does the child seem not to understand you and other adults, or other children? Is the child always the same, or can they sometimes speak more clearly than at other times? Can they manage some activities in school better than others? Are they better in a group or alone?

When you are speaking to the child, do you find yourself changing what you wanted to say so that they can understand you better?

Curriculum documents can be helpful in identifying how communication may be breaking down. For example, the English curriculum (in England) requires children to be able to:

1. listen, understand and respond to others and, when speaking to:
2. speak with clear diction and appropriate intonation;
3. choose words with precision;
4. organise what they say;
5. focus on the main point(s);
6. include relevant detail;
7. take into account the needs of their listeners.

   (Department for Education and Employment and Qualifications and
   Curriculum Authority 1999: 45)

By taking examples of language in the classroom, it is possible to see whether a child seems to have particular difficulty with any of these aspects of language.

The more questions that are asked about a child's communication, the more it should be possible to see whether there is indeed a difficulty and what their needs are. One of the most common ways of doing this is to compare children. Can a particular child do the same as others under similar circumstances? Teachers and parents often use this approach. For parents, if their child cannot do what their other children did at the same age, they may begin to worry. Parents also compare their children with others outside the family.

Although too much of this sort of comparison is not good as we know that children vary enormously in all aspects of their development, it is inevitable that comparisons are made. It can sometimes be the 'yardstick' for deciding whether a child may need some help. Teachers, of course, do this too. They are aware of the patterns of child development. They know that there is a very wide range of what might be considered 'normal'. They also know from experience when a child is very different from the others and when that difference seems to get in the way of a child's ability to learn in school.

It will be important to see whether the child's ability to communicate, either to understand or to express themselves, seems to prevent them from learning. We need to consider whether their opportunities in the curriculum seem to be disadvantaged by their language. Further, their apparent difficulties in communication may affect their relationships with other children, or with the adults in school. Their behaviour may be considered difficult if they fail to follow instructions or can't make themselves understood. This may affect their learning in many different ways.

Even when adjustments have been made, perhaps to the way the teacher talks to the child, or to the type of materials that are used to support the child's learning, the child may still seem to have difficulties. This may lead a teacher to consider the possibility of a specific speech or language need. At this stage, it does not matter what the difficulty is called. It is important, however, to describe it in as much detail as possible and to clarify what happens when the child tries to understand or to say things. A detailed description will help to determine where the difficulties lie, which will be important in deciding where to start helping.

Listening to the child

Understanding what a child says may be difficult for several reasons. It often takes some time for an adult to get used to a child. Teachers know that children's speech always seems to improve as they get to know them, although it is more likely that it is the adult who has 'improved'. They have learned to understand the child. However, the child's speech may be particularly unintelligible to a number of people, although fortunately family members can often understand the child. One point to remember is that a child's ability or wish to communicate is not always related in the most expected way to their intelligibility. For example, some children who are very difficult to understand will talk a great deal and will make every effort to communicate. Others may be reticent and talk very little. Some children who talk very little may be very responsive. Those who talk a lot may not be the best listeners. Some children may use physical ways of expressing themselves and may gain a reputation for being rough with other children. A child who does not understand what is said may appear to be disobedient. All of these will need to be considered in examining the nature of a child's speech or language difficulty. In the classroom, it is important to note whether a child is active or responsive in communicating, or both.

Firstly, a child may seem to have particular difficulties with speech sounds. They may miss the ends off words, they may substitute sounds or may use very distorted sounds. This is often most apparent in conversation. When there are no clues to the topic it can be very difficult to understand what the child is saying. It is fairly easy to see how these sort of problems arise if a child has a physical or structural problem. For example, a child with no front teeth may find 's' sounds difficult. A child who has a problem with movement, such as results sometimes from cerebral palsy, may not be able to make accurate tongue or lip movements and may not be able to control their breathing well enough to produce clear speech. A hearing loss may affect the child's response to sounds and may lead to distorted speech. However, there are also children who appear to have no structural problems in their mouth, no serious hearing problems or no obvious difficulties in making movements, yet their attempts to communicate are still difficult to understand. For some reason, they have a specific difficulty in learning to talk but may develop satisfactorily in other ways.

You will remember from the discussion on language development in Chapter 1 that, at certain stages, children may use one word form for many. For example, a child may say 'dee' for *tea*, *sea*, and *key* as well as for the letter *D*. Other children may use very few consonant sounds. They may say 'oo' for *look*; 'o' for *sock*, for *watch* and for *dog*. It is very difficult to understand them. Some children do not grow out of these immature speech patterns. They continue to use a restricted number of sounds in their speech and are often described as having a phonological difficulty. The problem lies in their inability to produce enough different sounds to distinguish between words. They have a difficulty with speech, but because the problem with speech sounds can affect the meaning of what the child tries to say, this type of problem can also be considered to be a language difficulty.

A problem at the phonological level can affect the production of word endings so that grammar (syntax) is inappropriate and meaning is therefore affected. Problems with grammar or meaning may make it very difficult to understand what a child is saying. Think of the relatively simple example of a child unable to produce 's' or 'z' sounds. This means that plurals cannot be conveyed. If the child misses all word endings, then this will make even more grammatical differences and the child will not be able to express meanings clearly. Problems in conveying meaning may affect the child's ability to use relevant language for a variety of situations and people.

Look at this short example from a four-year-old boy: 'me o de hwee me o de dwing'. Try to say it. Without knowing anything about the context, it is almost impossible to know what the child is talking about. Within the total context of a situation, it was possible to translate the utterance as, '*me don't get sweets me only get drinks*'. The child was talking about what he did when he went to a football match with his father.

If we go through the utterance we can see that the main obstacle to intelligibility is the boy's use of sounds. The word *don't* is represented only by the vowel 'o': 'd' replaces 'g' in *get*; 'hw' is substituted for 'sw' in *sweets*; 'dr' at the beginning of *drinks* is replaced by 'dw'; the final 's' signifying a plural at the end of *sweets* and *drinks* is omitted. The word *only* lacks its final syllable. There are also grammatical differences between this and adult speech: 'me' is used instead of 'I'. This brief example shows how the complex interactions between the different aspects of sounds and grammar in language can be affected in a child and can seriously impair communication. However, the child knew exactly what he wanted to say. The listener had a problem.

We can see that a breakdown in communication can occur at many different levels: the sounds, grammar, semantics (including vocabulary), pragmatics. Comprehension of language as well as expression may be affected. If a child is not understanding adequately, expressive language may be limited to short utterances which the child uses appropriately or it may comprise long adult-like sentences which are empty of meaning and function as the child is merely echoing language heard from others, without understanding.

Ways of thinking about language difficulty

Language difficulties can be viewed from a number of points of view and indeed, it is useful to take different perspectives if we are to try to understand them. The first perspective uses information from what we can see and what we can hear. It is based on observations of behaviour and analysis of language. Next, we consider the need to approach a difficulty from a consideration of possible influences on it. Thirdly, we view language and speech difficulties from a 'processing' perspective which looks at how sensory and perceptual mechanisms might affect language skills. Here, we introduce the main ideas of these approaches and further detail will be discussed in later chapters.

Communicative behaviour

In Chapter 1 we presented the components of language as content, form and function or use. Usually, as a child develops, these three components overlap and integrate. Each is essential for effective communication through language. We can take examples of language and employ Bloom and Lahey's model (1978) to look at what happens when one or more of the components does not develop for some reason. We might say that a language or a speech difficulty becomes apparent when there is a disruption within a component of the model or in the integration of content, form and use. There may therefore be difficulties with ideas, with the language structure or in learning to use language which is appropriate for the linguistic community.

Of course, a language problem rarely falls so neatly into these categories. Each component of language depends upon, and integrates with, the others and this will usually be the case when a child has difficulty with language. For example, children with problems of meaning or content frequently have difficulties with form because conceptual development is necessary in order to learn about form and about how to use form as a means for social interaction (Lahey 1988). Children who do not understand the meanings of words or who cannot use the appropriate words for a situation may have great difficulties in social communication with other children or with adults. The model can be helpful in describing the area of language in which the problem predominantly lies or it can focus our attention on examples of language which present problems to the child and others with whom they try to communicate.

Bloom and Lahey look at language from a linguistic point of view. In order to decide whether the content, the form or the function of language is disrupted, we need to take examples of the language and analyse them. We need to examine the content, the grammar and sounds and the way in which the language is used, the function. Linguistic analysis has given us many new insights into language difficulties, allowing us to look in some detail at the particular level of language which is problematic. Even without very much training in linguistic analysis it is possible to gain some idea of where difficulties lie, by using the descriptions of language employed in curriculum documents. If we go back to the examples given earlier from the English curriculum (p.25) we can use the requirements to gain a general picture of a child's spoken language skills. Whenever a child's language is of concern, try to say, with some precision, whether the child is able to:

- 'speak with clear diction and appropriate intonation'. Is the child generally easy to understand or are sounds confused and unclear?

- 'choose words with precision'. Is there a detectable development in vocabulary over time so that the child is heard to use the same word in different contexts or new words for different purposes?

- 'organise what they say'. Can the child use different 'parts of speech' appropriately – for example, tenses of verbs, plurals, pronouns? Are words in the right order? Are ideas in a logical order?

- 'focus on the main point(s)'; include relevant detail; take into account the needs of their listeners. In order to determine these, it will be necessary to listen to a child in a variety of settings and situations. If the child is unable to fulfil these expectations, is it because they do not have the vocabulary, the appropriate sentence structures or do not seem to know what to say, to whom and when?

- 'listen, understand and respond to others'. Curriculum documents usually place these skills last in the list and refer to 'speaking and listening' or 'talking and listening'. They should probably be considered first as they suggest whether or not a child is able to understand. We will look at this in greater detail in the next chapter.

Although the main emphasis will be on communication through language, we need to look at other areas of development too. A consideration of language difficulties within this framework will involve the collection of information about things that a child can and cannot do. In particular, in the classroom, it will involve the collection of information about how the child relates to children and adults, and how the child copes with day-to-day activities in school. There is a growing body of research suggesting that language and behaviour difficulties are linked. Children who experience speech or language difficulties in their early years have been found to be at risk of developing behaviour difficulties later (Stevenson *et al.* 1985). A study by Lindsay and Dockrell (2000) of 69 children aged 7–8 years with specific speech and language difficulties found a higher prevalence of behaviour difficulties than would be expected in a typically developing group of children of the same age.

Perhaps it is not surprising that children with difficulties in communication are also found to have lower self-esteem and more problems in making social relationships than their peers. All of this suggests that it is important to be alert to children who show behaviour difficulties or who may not be well accepted by other children. These may in fact be a sign that the child has language and communication needs.

The collection of information about the child's speech and language in the classroom and the language used by the adults and other children with the child will be particularly important. (See Chapter 10 for a format for doing this). By careful recording and analysis of the behaviour and when it occurs, we should be able to identify the area or areas of speech and/or language that hinder communication.

Consideration of language in these terms can be useful in identifying specific areas of difficulty. However, a linguistic perspective only gives us one view. It gives, perhaps, the most obvious one, the part that we can see or hear when we engage in conversation with a child. If we are to find ways of helping children, we need to look further, and from another perspective.

Causes and influences

At the same time as examining what we can see and hear, we will be asking ourselves 'why?' We need to consider whether there are any obvious reasons for these particular characteristics of speech or language. Are there any physical or medical conditions which may have contributed or which may be maintaining a child's difficulty? For example, in some children, hearing loss, associated with chronic coughs and colds, may be identified. Some children are particularly prone to infections of the ears, nose and throat. This is not to say that the hearing problems inevitably caused the difficulties. There would rarely be a single, simple cause. However, the effects of coughs and colds may have reacted with other things going on. A child may have missed school because of frequent infections so that learning opportunities were reduced or, even earlier in life, heavy colds may have prevented the child from hearing accurately. They may have failed to learn to listen. Sometimes parents describe early feeding difficulties, which may suggest that a child's mouth was not very well coordinated when he or she was a baby. Information about a child's early life would be important in the investigations of communication difficulty because it might be possible to take some action to make things better. Ear infections, for example, may respond to antibiotics. Surgery might be necessary if a child has a cleft lip or palate. In these examples, we would be utilising medical information to inform our discussions. It would be important to consider medical information and to keep it in mind as a possible influence on a child's development.

We would also need to consider the child's social and emotional experiences although, as with illnesses, we cannot say with absolute certainty how they are involved. Consider the example of a child who is the youngest of a large family – in some cases, a child will respond to this by developing very rapidly and speaking in a very mature way, to keep up with the rest of the family; in another case, the child may speak very little – everyone else speaks for them – or they may speak in a very immature way as the 'baby' of the family.

Nothing is straightforward and all behaviour is a response to very complex interactions and circumstances. Historically, ways of thinking which tend to focus on cause and effect have been influential in the study of problems of human communication, although it is probably true to say that their importance has diminished as the value of other frameworks has been realised. It is important to remember that there will rarely be a single, simple, cause of language disability and we must always consider a range of possible influences. We would agree with John Harris when he says that 'it is safer to focus on the specific pattern of abilities and disabilities shown by the child's assessment profile, rather than to seek explanations of *how* the child came to develop in a particular way' (Harris 1990: 225).

Linguistic and medical perspectives could be extremely helpful in trying to understand a child's communication needs. Neither of them on their own would be sufficient and we would still need to make other considerations. The same medical condition can give rise to different difficulties. Similar features of spoken language may have different underlying causes. Other frameworks may be useful in adding to our understanding and suggesting ways of helping.

A processing perspective

The third perspective which we will consider is based on attempts to understand how a child is processing language. This draws on ideas from the disciplines of neurology and cognitive psychology. These suggest ways in which the brain might be functioning. In Chapter 1 we suggested that perception and memory are important in developing speech and language. These 'cognitive processes' will determine how a person receives information, stores it and then organises it to produce or reproduce it. Working within such a framework will make us consider how the child uses its visual and auditory senses and perceptual processes. For example, a child may not be able to hear very well and therefore the 'input' of sound may be imperfect. Other children, even though they can hear adequately, have difficulties in discriminating between sounds or perceiving them in the right order (sequence). Perception is about the way the senses, of vision, hearing and touch, are used to understand our environment. The difficulties of some children are thought to lie in perceptual processes. Poor control of attention may affect the amount of information a child receives. If, for some reason, they do not take in, then memorise or store information correctly, this will mean that they cannot reproduce it correctly.

However, even if they receive information accurately and memorise it, a child may have difficulties in organising or producing sounds or words in the way they are heard. Their 'motor planning' or 'motor programming' processes may be a source of difficulty; their organisation of movements may be weak. A language processing perspective may suggest to us why a child cannot speak clearly. This will be very important as, although two children may speak in similar ways, it may be for very different reasons. One may not perceive sounds accurately and so is only able to repeat the 'faulty' sounds they have heard. Another may perceive very well but not be able to coordinate movements well enough to make the same sounds that they hear.

In order to work from this perspective, we would need to carry out a range of tasks with a child and attempt to identify as precisely as possible where an individual child was having difficulties.

Each of the frameworks described above focuses on the child and what he or she can and cannot do. They tend to be 'problem-focused' frameworks. Although it is important to analyse and describe in great detail what is happening, we must remember that communication is never about a single, isolated individual. Communication is, by definition, about interaction and the context in which it takes place. It will always be necessary to look at the communicative attempts of others around a child and to consider the expectations they have and the demands they are making.

Conclusion

We have provided a broad overview of how language difficulties may be apparent and some of the perspectives we can take on them. Although there are many different views and terminology may lack precision, we hope that we have made a convincing case for examining language in more detail. Language is one of the most important factors in developing inclusive practice. Differences in understanding and using language can quickly create problems which potentially exclude people from social and learning opportunities. Most people have experienced situations where they did not understand what was going on, or could not ask for what they wanted, perhaps because they were out of their familiar surroundings, where a different language was spoken. This perhaps gives some idea of the experiences of children who may be learning English as an additional language or have particular difficulties in learning language.

Practitioners in schools are in an excellent position to make observations of children and to provide examples of communication in the classroom. It is the responsibility of adults to ensure that the classroom environment engages children in learning and so the focus is not only the language of the children but also the communication skills of the adults.

In the next chapters, we look at some specific aspects of language difficulty and some possible explanations for them. This will help practitioners to identify needs with more precision, and therefore to plan more appropriate support for children.

Further reading

Dockrell, J. and Messer, D. (1999) *Children's Language and Communication Difficulties: Understanding, Identification and Intervention.* London: Cassell.

Frederickson, N. and Cline, T. (2002) *Special Educational Needs: Inclusion and Diversity.* Buckingham: Open University Press.

Martin, D. (2000) *Teaching Children with Speech and Language Difficulties.* London: David Fulton Publishers.

Chapter 3

Speech difficulties

Introduction

So far we have argued that there are different ways of understanding and talking about speech and language, depending on whether the approach is linguistic, psychological or educational. Furthermore, there are differences in how we describe difficulties in speech and language, and there is controversy about how we quantify and categorise these difficulties in children and young people. In the following chapters we explore the nature of speech and language in more depth and focus on difficulties in speech, grammar, meaning and language in use as well as literacy.

In this chapter we focus on difficulties in speech. There is a range of speech difficulties which occur in children and young people and research findings help to explain their nature and causes. The implications of these findings are discussed with particular attention to assessment of speech difficulties and intervention approaches. The wider management of pupils with speech difficulties involves parents and other professionals. When speech is not feasible, other communication systems, such as alternative and augmented systems, need to be considered and are briefly explored here.

Perceptions of speech difficulties

When we communicate with an individual who has a speech difficulty, we may become involved in gauging the extent to which the difficulty is affecting the quality of the communication. We may become more concerned about how the person is speaking to us than by what he or she is saying. This is the first stage of an assessment of a speech difficulty. When communication is hindered because of someone's speech difficulty then this is cause for concern.

Emotional, social and behavioural difficulties are often associated with preschool and school-aged children with severe speech difficulties. They may become extremely frustrated due to difficulties in communication.

Children and young people with these difficulties may show reluctance or withdrawal from public communication. They may also have dramatic stress-related reactions to communicative situations. Parents and teachers need to be sensitive and aware of this aspect of speech difficulties and seek strategies to support independent intelligible communication for learners with speech difficulties.

There is some evidence of peer group reactions to children who have speech difficulties. In classrooms, peers embark on communicating with children who have speech difficulties but then as they receive either no response or a response which they have difficulty understanding, they react in one of two ways. They either dominate communication, giving their partner little opportunity or need to reply, or they stop communicating altogether and continue the activity in silence (Lewis 1990). Older pupils in language units have reported that they feel that their peers and teachers in the mainstream school perceive them as having additional difficulties, such as learning difficulties. Peers call them names to this effect. Teachers report that they are not trained to teach pupils with a range of difficulties (Sinclair Taylor 1995). There are implications for social as well as academic development of pupils with speech difficulties within the peer group and school, particularly those with long-term speech difficulties.

In most cases with young children, parents or main caregivers will be the first adults to notice that communication is disturbed by the child's speech difficulty. However, in some cases the class teacher may be the first adult who notices, based on the fact that most four-year-olds are 90 per cent intelligible to strangers (cited in Law *et al.* 2000: 18). Often parents, caregivers and teachers who communicate a great deal with the young person will report that they no longer notice the speech difficulty because they have 'tuned in' to the child's way of speaking. While this may relieve some of the immediate frustrations for both child and adult, the child will face communication difficulties each time they speak to an unfamiliar person.

The importance of appreciating the social and emotional effects of speech difficulties on children cannot be overestimated. Although not all children and young people who have speech difficulties have negative perceptions of their speech, for those individuals who have, there are substantial implications for their learning which the family and the practitioner should be aware of. For example, increased anxiety, low self-esteem, feelings of alienation and rejection from the peer group will all reduce pupils' readiness to learn. One of the key roles of family and practitioners is to support the individual with speech difficulties in these areas of social and emotional development (see Chapter 9).

Let us now consider the nature of speech, and speech difficulties.

Speech

Speech is a dual system: it is a motor skill and a mode of language expression, articulation and phonology. **Articulation** is a particular set of motor skill learning where moving the speech articulators in our mouths in rapid, precise and coordinated sequences becomes automatic. Studying articulation is called *phonetics*. The phonetic aspect of speech includes speech sounds and also the *volume, rhythm* and *musicality* of what we say. Speech sounds can be segmented in various ways: into the parts of their articulation and into consonants and vowels. By contrast, volume, rhythm and musicality – pitch and intonation – are non-segmental aspects which cannot easily be segmented. They are also known as the *prosody* of speech.

Phonology is the meaning level of speech. It refers 'to all the sound-related aspects of language, knowledge and behaviour' (Watson 1991: 26). A central aspect of phonology is the speech sound system, where speech sounds are organised into sequences to make words, and have meaning attributed to them to make meaningful sound contrasts which change word meaning; for example, contrast *p* and *t*: pill/till, cap/cat, caper/cater. Prosodic aspects of speech are also phonological when they influence the meaning of the whole utterance; for example a rising intonation can mean questioning, loudness can mean anger, quietness can mean intimacy.

In many cases only the articulatory and segmental features of speech are considered when assessing speech difficulties. The other prosodic aspects of speech are not investigated. Yet individuals can show difficulties with prosody which affect their communication, and this is particularly linked with difficulties using language appropriately. We discuss this later.

Linguistic minority groups

Children from linguistic minority communities who are developing two speech sound systems usually cope well when exposed to two languages during the early years of their development. A multilingual environment is not in itself a problem. Some bilingual children may show confusions between the two speech sound systems, and use a speech sound contrast from one language in the system of the other. The two systems usually sort themselves out within a few years. However, children who are having difficulties with their speech development for whatever reason may present problems in one or both languages and will need to be assessed in both languages (Duncan 1989).

Bilingual children who present with speech difficulties in both languages can show speech improvement in both languages even though intervention is only given in one language. In a case study of a bilingual Panjabi-English child with inconsistent speech difficulties in both languages, a phonological intervention approach improved the child's speech in both languages even though intervention had only been given in English (Holm and Dodd 1999).

Speech difficulties

Let us consider what we mean by *speech difficulties*. Probably the most obvious manifestation of a speech difficulty will be a lack of *intelligibility*. Speech may be unintelligible because sounds are omitted, substituted or distorted. The difficulty may be at an articulatory or a phonological level, or both, and segmental and/or prosodic elements of speech may be affected. That is, there may be problems at the sound production level as well as accompanying problems of pitch, voice control and resonance.

An articulation problem means that speech difficulties are due to the inadequate motor skills in speech sound production. A phonological difficulty means that the child's development of the meaningful use of speech sounds has in some way become idiosyncratic. There is usually overlap between the development of articulation skills and phonology, the meaningful contrast of speech sounds. The distinction between an articulation difficulty and a phonological one is important because it reflects the interpretation of the nature of speech difficulties and also the approach taken in intervention. We return to this topic later in the chapter.

Causes of articulatory difficulties may lie in physical reasons such as problems with the mouth structure, as in the case of a child with cleft lip and palate. There may be neurological reasons affecting oral movement, associated with cerebral palsy, or there may be sensory reasons, such as hearing impairment. With phonological difficulty there is often no obvious cause to explain unintelligibility and the restricted speech sound system.

Delay or difficulty?

Speech difficulty indicates that the child's speech and language development is *different* from what you would expect for the child's chronological or mental age, within the social context of the child's development. We will consider the nature of speech difficulties within a developmental framework.

For some children their speech difficulties have resolved themselves while they are still in primary school. It could be said that that they seem 'to grow out of it'. For other children their speech difficulties resolve after intervention and for a small group of children their speech difficulties do not completely resolve even in adulthood, despite many years of intervention.

Ingram (1989) interprets speech, or more accurately, *phonological*, difficulties by identifying patterns of speech development which most children seem to display, so-called normal speech development and then uses it as a basis for comparison for other patterns of speech development. Delayed phonological development would be seen in children who seem to be following a similar course of speech development as most children but more slowly, such as the child who may be five years old but has the speech patterns displayed by most four-year-olds.

He then identifies two groups of children who have phonological difficulties. There are those children who seem to follow a developmental pattern similar to that of most children but who do not drop certain early speech patterns. They maintain these patterns alongside more advanced ones so that their speech is different from most other children of their age. They may, for example, be able to produce relatively mature speech patterns but still have obvious immaturities in their speech. The other group of children who have substantial speech difficulties are thought to develop speech in a unique way, quite differently from most children. This view, held by many people, may not be entirely justified. The more researchers look at the speech of these children, the more often they find that what was previously identified as 'unique' development occurs in some typically developing children, those without speech difficulties. Ingram has used the term 'deviant' speech while others, teachers and speech and language therapists in the UK, usually refer to 'severe speech difficulties'.

Characteristics of children with speech difficulties

We need to consider the broad pattern of general development in children described as having delayed speech development. Many of these children share similar characteristics in their overall development. One group usually seem to have age-appropriate play and understanding of language with specific speech delay. For example, they often have a history of feeding difficulties as babies and may continue to be finicky about food. They may have had frequent coughs and colds in their preschool years. These difficulties may persist in some children in the early school years, reducing their overall alertness and attentiveness in class, and they will need careful monitoring for both speech development and general learning. In contrast, there are children with speech difficulties who also show general delay across all aspects of development, including attention difficulties. This developmental pattern contrasts with children who seem only to have difficulties in speech development, so-called 'specific' speech delay.

It is important to note that poor speech intelligibility often makes it difficult to assess whether other aspects of language, such as grammar and vocabulary, are affected. As intelligibility improves other language difficulties may become apparent.

The speech of children with severe speech difficulties, as described above by Ingram, lies within a developmental framework. However, there is also a small group of children whose speech lies outside the developmental framework because their difficulties arise from medical or neurological factors, which are described now.

Approaches to speech difficulties

Medical, linguistic and psycholinguistic approaches are helpful for thinking about speech difficulties and understanding speech difficulties in social and educational contexts.

A medical approach

A medical approach to speech difficulties emphasises structural, sensory and genetic problems. Information about these factors is important because medical management may influence later development as well as teaching and intervention. In some cases medical management may control the problem, as for example when antibiotics are given for recurrent colds and ear infections. In other cases, when there are structural abnormalities such as a cleft lip and palate, or severe, chronic middle ear infections, the problem may be resolved by surgery. Recent studies suggest that some severe speech difficulties are hereditary and occur in families (Pembry 1992). Practitioners in education need to be informed about medical problems in a child's history because of the possible influences on development and learning. It is also important to know of any previous or ongoing medical involvement.

Medical information with neurological implications is also important for children with speech difficulties. Cases of neurological damage include head injury in an accident and brain damage before, during or soon after birth.

While some children recover, others may experience lifelong physical disabilities with associated speech difficulties. Neurological disease includes brain tumours and infectious diseases such as meningitis. Speech difficulties for these children may be progressive so that there will be a deterioration over time. Speech difficulties of neurological origin are known as *dysarthrias*. They are usually characterised by slurred articulation caused by difficulties in motor skills and coordination. On the other hand, speech may be tense and staccato due to increased muscle tone. Breathing and eating patterns may also be affected. Educational implications for these children suggest that they may have to communicate and access the curriculum through non-speech systems, such as signing, computer-aided communication or display boards.

There is a further speech difficulty, *dyspraxia*, which is thought to be due to immature neural development. It is usually manifested by clumsiness because of difficulties in coordination, which gives it its other name: *Developmental Coordination Difficulty* (DCD). Neural development may mature and there may be some improvement in coordination. Verbal dyspraxia affects speech and is characterised by unpredictable, inconsistent and unintelligible speech patterns. There may also be difficulties in language and literacy skills.

There are identifiable speech difficulties for children with chronic and recurring ear infections which leave them with fluctuating or moderate hearing loss. A familiar example concerns difficulties in hearing high frequencies and usually results in the absence of fricative sounds, (such as *f, v, s, z*) and sounds at the end of words. However, there are also children with *sensory-neural type deafness* who may have longer-term problems, which may or may not respond to medical or surgical intervention. They may be provided with other specialist help with their education from teachers of the deaf and speech and language therapists.

Finally, difficulties with voicing, *dysphonia*, may have a physical cause. Dysphonia may be caused by a congenital malformation of the vocal cords or by straining the voice, such as by shouting. Sometimes, the cause may not be physical but more physiological or psychological, as when an adolescent boy's voice does not break, or when one loses one's voice through stress. Advice and intervention from a speech and language therapist can improve most of these difficulties.

A linguistic approach

In a linguistic approach to understanding speech difficulties two frameworks are presented which are in popular practice: error analysis and the natural phonology. These frameworks, in very different ways, explain how speech develops in the child and try to account for patterns of difficulty. They provide the basis for the assessment and intervention procedures which have been developed for speech difficulties.

Error analysis

Error analysis is the traditional framework for explaining and classifying speech 'defects' and difficulties, proposed by two American speech pathologists Van Riper and Irwin (1958). It sees speech development as progressing from sound to sound until the child has the full repertoire of adult sounds and uses them correctly. Consequently, speech difficulties are interpreted as the child selecting and using the 'wrong' sound, hence the name 'error' analysis. 'Remediation' focuses on teaching the child to produce the 'right' sound and to practise it correctly in the various places in words. An example of an error analysis of an articulation difficulty is the so-called 'slushy s' where the 's' sound is produced with the air being released along the sides of the mouth rather than along the midline. In English, the meaning of words with this unusual pronunciation is usually not affected. A programme of raising the individual's awareness of the 'slushy s' together with articulation exercises to facilitate air release along the midline of the mouth would usually be an effective approach to improving this articulation difficulty.

The limitation of error analysis is that it understands speech only as a set of motor skills. Studies of children's speech development show that children do not learn speech sounds individually but within a system of making sounds meaningful. It seems likely that children learn *distinctive articulation features* which are common to a number of sounds, for example lip closure, as in sounds *p, b, m*, and the friction found in sounds such as *s, z, f, v, sh*. Additionally, their speech development will be linked with their motor maturation, their developing auditory perception and their overall cognitive and conceptual functioning. Moreover, the need to express clear meanings encourages them to make contrasts between speech sounds and this linguistic motivation is the driving force in their phonological development. For example, the need to articulate the sounds *p* and *t* differently is because they can be used in words to make different meanings.

Error analysis cannot grasp the linguistic nature of the development of phonology, which is about sounds in the meaningful context of language. Despite this, an articulatory approach to phonological development continues to be popular with some speech and language therapists and educationists. Error analysis is the basis for a number of commercial assessments, such as *The Edinburgh Articulation Test* (Anthony *et al.* 1971). It is important that practitioners in their work with children bear in mind the linguistic nature of speech sounds; that they function within a system and not in isolation.

Natural phonology

Natural phonology, as put forward by Stampe (1972), has grown from the idea that children develop speech through *phonological processes* which function on the whole emerging speech sound system through words. Phonological processes are linked with developing motor control and auditory perception which constrain and shape the developing phonological system. Phonological processes control all the speech sounds in a word. For example, for ease in motor skills, sounds may be harmonised (consonant harmony) in a word, so that *dog* becomes *dod* or *gog*, or clusters of sounds may be reduced (cluster reduction) so that *spade* becomes *pade* and *crash* becomes *cash*. The shape of the whole word can be influenced when the weakly stressed syllable, which would be less easily perceived, is deleted (weak syllable deletion), for example, *balloon* becomes *boon*, and *tomato* becomes *mato*. Two very common processes in children's phonological development are called 'fronting' and 'backing' where many speech sounds are articulated mainly at the 'front' (behind the teeth) or at the 'back' of the mouth. An example of 'fronting' is when *come and get my cup* becomes *tum an det my tup*. An example of 'backing' would be that *that's my bike* becomes *ga gy gike*. The implications for assessment and intervention are that the child's phonological system is approached as a whole and the child is encouraged to develop through the processes towards a full speech sound system.

There are limitations to the natural phonology approach to speech difficulties. This approach offers a description of phonological patterns and processes which children develop, and offers an explanation for delayed and atypical speech development. However, it does not explore the relationship between phonology and articulation. Nor does it explain how the child interacts with phonological information, or manages and manipulates speech sound information. It is this failure that has led to the emergence of the cognitive psycholinguistic approach.

A psycholinguistic approach

The psycholinguistic approach explores how phonological information is handled by underlying cognitive and linguistic processing and tries to identify at what level the processing breaks down, giving rise to speech difficulties. In Chapter 1 we briefly described a cognitive approach to language, in terms of perception, storage, access, retrieval and output. With specific reference to speech, Stackhouse and Wells (1997) have developed a speech processing model within a cognitive approach. Their model explains speech processing by suggesting that the brain receives speech input through auditory perception, and recognises it as a word with (or without) meaning. The brain stores speech (word) information in representations of phonological knowledge, which include information about the speech sound sequence, e.g. the onset and coda. This knowledge is also known as phonological awareness. Processes in the brain access and retrieve knowledge of phonological representations and transform it into output motor patterns which produce speech articulation, or writing.

On the basis of articulatory and phonological assessment, it would be likely that we could identify where the point of difficulty in speech processing occurs. The child's speech processing strengths would also be identified through these tasks and intervention would be focused on developing the areas of processing difficulty, based usually on the child's areas of ability. There are several aspects of speech processing which include auditory discrimination and segmenting words into syllables and sounds (Stackhouse and Wells 1997). For example, children with speech difficulties might have difficulty perceiving differences between words which have similarities in sound sequences, such as *lots* and *lost*. They might be unable to segment a two-syllable word, or identify the first or last sounds in a word. They might not be able to identify words which rhyme or produce words which rhyme. They may produce instead words which begin with the same sound or words which are close in meaning. For example, in a task that asks the child to find a rhyme for *man*, rather than offering *can, ban,* or *chan*, the child might say *mouse,* (same onset as *man*) or *boy* (same semantic field as *man*) (Stackhouse and Wells 1993). In everyday activities for these children, this would mean that I-spy games would be very difficult, as well as clapping rhythms or appreciating rhyming aspects of poetry and song.

Depending on the nature of the difficulty, the child may show breakdown at one or more levels of speech processing. For example, it may be possible to have difficulties only in organising speech output. Usually, there is an interrelationship between all levels of processing so that there is feedback into the speech sound system, enabling a certain amount of monitoring at a non-conscious level. For this reason it may be advantageous to work on aspects of input and output at the same time, rather than separate the two aspects completely.

A psycholinguistic approach to speech difficulties shows the association between speech processing and processing the written form of language.

Difficulties with reading, writing and spelling are discussed in the next chapter. Many practitioners in education work within the cognitive framework of learning and would find a great deal that is familiar in the psycholinguistic approach to speech difficulties. This approach allows for individual, task-based programmes to be developed which could be jointly planned by teacher and therapist. It also allows for group-based support and intervention.

An educational approach

An educational approach seeks to understand and support learning for pupils who have speech difficulties, either as delayed development or as more substantial difficulties. The educational approach, to be optimally effective, needs to draw on information about the children concerned from the medical, linguistic and psycholinguistic approaches. To accomplish this, teachers need to liaise and collaborate with important others, such as parents, SENCOs and speech and language therapists.

There are three main aspects of the educational approach for children with speech difficulties: to contribute to assessment; to support learning and develop management strategies for speech difficulties; and to support social and emotional development when it is affected as a result of speech difficulties.

Assessment

The teacher may be the first adult outside the family who has to communicate in an important way with the child with speech difficulties. The decision to raise her/his concern about the child with others may depend on awareness of typical speech development, unintelligibility, observation of the child's general developmental skills and learning, as well as observation of communication with peers.

To support pupils with speech difficulties in class, teachers need to be aware that speech difficulties are likely to be associated with difficulties learning new vocabulary, grammatical word endings, and literacy difficulties. Effective support can be given at a whole-class level to young children through phonological awareness approaches, and building positive supportive links between speech and literacy. For older learners, explicit teaching of semantic, phonological and grammatical aspects of new vocabulary is helpful, e.g. raising phonological awareness about word segmentation into syllables, onsets, rimes and codas, and identifying semantic associations. Additional communication may need to be considered as a support for severely unintelligible children, such as a signing system like Makaton (Walker 1978) or a picture board. Teachers and pupils would need to be involved in using it if the child is to use it effectively. Associated difficulties with literacy often occur in learners with speech difficulties and teachers need to be alert to this.

Support and intervention

There are approaches to support and intervention which are based on developing children's phonological awareness, e.g. metaphonological approaches such as 'Metaphon' (Howell and Dean 1994, Dean et al. 1990). Metaphonological approaches can be combined with articulation-based approaches which encourage children to develop speech motor skills, such as the Nuffield programme.

One recent study compared the effectiveness of these two approaches with preschool children with developmental phonological difficulties (Hesketh et al. 2000: Adams et al. 2000). Children were given intervention in groups and individually. Articulation-based intervention focused on the production of the children's problematic speech sounds in isolation, in CV and VC combinations and later in words and sentences. In contrast, the metaphonological-based programme worked on general phonological awareness and specific awareness tasks involving their target speech sounds or processes, such as rhyming, syllable clapping, alliteration and blending.

Producing the target speech sounds was not done until the last two weeks of the programme. The children's speech in both groups improved similarly. Although the speech of the children in the articulation-based group seemed to have changed more, the speech of the children in the metaphonological group continued to make more long-term change. The implications of these findings suggest that class or group phonological awareness work, planned by teachers and therapists, can significantly improve speech difficulties in children.

Speech difficulties may occur on their own in the language system of a child and they may occur together with difficulties in other levels of language. Stammering and speech sounds and grammar (phonological-syntactic) difficulties are two examples.

Stammering

Stammering or stuttering (used interchangeably and not two different types of difficulty) is a difficulty in the rhythm of spoken language, so-called *disfluency*. Stammering can involve repetitions of syllables or sounds, or silent blocks on some articulations. People who stammer often have associated feelings and attitudes which may influence the nature of the difficulty and intervention. Stammering may also mask a difficulty in another level of language which may only become apparent after extensive assessment or as the stammering improves. For example, individuals may also have phonological difficulties and/or difficulties with grammar.

It is important to bear in mind that in the course of development most children pass through a phase of disfluency, usually between two and four years of age and it usually resolves by five years.

Speech sounds and grammar difficulties

A speech difficulty may affect the grammar of an utterance, particularly at the level of word endings. For example, the speech sounds, 's' and 'z' are used to signal a variety of grammatical features, such as plurality (as in *rats, shoes*), third person singular (as in *walks, runs*) and possession (as in *lamb's, girl's*). Children who have difficulty with these two sounds may, therefore, also have difficulty signalling these grammatical features even though they may be aware of them. However, there may be some children who do not signal these word endings even though they can produce 's' and 'z' in word final positions in words. These children would have a grammatical, not a speech, difficulty.

Describing speech

Speech difficulties are described and explained in different ways. Grunwell (1987: 44) describes one approach: 'In literate societies, the non-specialist is often able to describe the specific "defects" of speech in terms of the "sounds" or "letters" that are mispronounced'. This approach assumes that 'sounds' and 'letters' are synonymous and interchangeable, which they are not. Phoneticians and others, such as speech and language therapists, use the International Phonetic Alphabet (IPA). The IPA is an alphabet of all the speech sounds – consonants and vowels – used in the known languages of the world. The IPA also has symbols for vocal change, such as pitch and intonation. Although some of the IPA symbols resemble English letters there are many symbols which do not. The IPA is also used by speech and language therapists, to describe speech sounds produced by individuals with speech difficulties.

Each symbol in the IPA represents a sound so that a sequence of IPA symbols represents the actual sequence of pronounced sounds. The primary relevance of the IPA to those involved with children with speech and language difficulties is that it is a means of describing as accurately as possible the children's speech sounds. Description provides a form of analysis for unusual speech sounds, thus moving them from the arena of being 'funny', 'strange', 'odd', to being analysable and understandable.

While it is important that teachers are acquainted with the IPA so that they are able to understand better the children's speech difficulties and to appreciate the speech and language therapists' perspective, it is unlikely to be a useful or appropriate tool for them in describing pupils' speech.

The context of the speech sound

A speech sound can be pronounced in four linguistic contexts: on its own, in a word, in a syllable and in connected speech. These contexts influence the speech sound.

In isolation: Pronouncing a speech sound on its own – in isolation – is a contrived context because it is not a natural speaking context and the value of the information obtained about the production – articulation – of the speech sound must be questioned. Some children can pronounce a speech sound, such as 'l' on its own but are unable to pronounce it in words such as *leg, slow, filler*. We can conclude that these children have the coordination to articulate the speech sound but are not incorporating it into their speech. Yet there are assessment procedures which include this. We must also consider the way in which speech sounds in isolation are elicited. This is usually done by imitation of the adult or by reading the nearest corresponding letter, in which case other skills are required which might disadvantage the child.

Other assessment procedures require that the speech sound is articulated at different speeds to measure the speed and accuracy of articulation which can be compared with some known measures. In connected speech articulatory rate is between 5.2 and 9.6 movements per second (Dalton and Hardcastle 1977: 43), which is about 1000 movements per minute. This information would be important because it would reveal that the child had some difficulties in the area of coordination of speech muscles.

In a word: Assessing the pronunciation of speech sounds in the context of a word is more natural but the other speech sounds in the word will influence the articulation of the targeted speech sound. For example, consider how you pronounce the 't' sound in the word *batman*. Most people would pronounce 't' like 'p' because of the influence of the lip closure from the following 'm'. Thus, the choice of words and the position within the word of the speech sounds which we wish the child to pronounce must be considered carefully. The child is usually required to name a picture, which demands few additional skills although words familiar to the child must be selected.

In a syllable: The syllable is the smallest natural linguistic context in which the speech sound occurs. Many speech assessments select single syllable words, where the targeted sound is either the initial or the final sound and thus only minimally influenced by other sounds.

In connected speech: Connected speech, as in ordinary conversational speech, is the most natural context for assessing children's speech sounds. The speech sounds are influenced by neighbouring sounds which need careful monitoring and analysis. One drawback with this form of assessment with children whose speech is difficult to understand is that, without any clear reference to the matters they are talking about, it is difficult for the adult to identify what words the child is pronouncing. Often a context must be established, such as talking about a shared picture, story or event in the child's day.

For a thorough analysis of the child's speech, speech samples should be tape-recorded and analysed at a later time to enable repeated checks of the child's pronunciations. It is best to collect tape-recorded speech samples from a variety of locations, such as at home and at different times in the school day. This is an opportunity for parents, teachers and speech and language therapists to work together.

Conclusion

In this chapter some of the aspects of speech and the nature of speech difficulties have been explored. There are typical features in speech development, that is phonological processes, which persist and inhibit further speech development in many children with speech difficulties. Speech assessment should aim to include speech samples from a variety of communication settings. Children developing bilingually who seem to have speech difficulties need to be assessed in both languages. Intervention in one language can improve speech intelligibility across both languages.

Discussions of the nature of speech difficulties have taken three perspectives; medical, linguistic and psycholinguistic. The linguistic and psycholinguistic approaches seem to have more influence on speech assessment and intervention in the classroom. The importance of an educational approach to speech difficulties is identified in terms of assessment, support and managing associated social and emotional difficulties. In the next chapter, literacy difficulties are discussed, which are widely perceived as associated with speech and language processing difficulties and are interpreted mainly from a psycholinguistic perspective.

Further reading

Stackhouse, J. and Wells, B. (1997) *Children's Speech and Literacy Difficulties: a Psycholinguistic Framework.* London: Whurr.

Chapter 4

Difficulties in reading, writing and spelling

Introduction

In the last chapter we explored the nature of speech and speech difficulties in the classroom and we suggested that there were close associations between the speech process and certain literacy skills. These associations become clear in some frameworks, particularly the cognitive, psycholinguistic framework. In this chapter we look at these associations in more detail as well as the links between literacy and the other aspects of language, such as grammar and meaning.

Studying literacy is a wide field. There are three broad approaches to literacy. Literacy is studied as a social practice, which people in communities use to shape their lives, to develop shared cognitions and to communicate values and beliefs. Another approach studies literacy as a vehicle for maintaining or challenging structures of power in societies; for example, studying access to literacy, how ideas are presented in texts and developing critical literacy. Thirdly, there is the approach we take here which investigates literacy as reading, writing and spelling skills. This 'technical' approach is also taken in education documents about literacy in the UK and in departments of education in many other countries.

Within a technical approach, literacy can be appreciated on two levels; for the individual and for society. The importance of literacy within society is reflected by the fact that it is used throughout the world as a measure of a society's maturity. The percentage of literate people within a society is a mark of the society's education. However, there are different criteria for measuring literacy, which undermine attempts to compare national literacy development. In some countries people's literacy development is measured by reading age/level, while in other countries it is measured by the number of years in formal education, possibly based on school attendance figures. In the UK, national literacy achievement is often taken as a measure of the effectiveness of the education system and consequently has become an issue of public interest and concern. Indications that there is a decline in literacy standards (however these may be measured) are often interpreted as a decline in the success of the wider educational system.

For example, in the UK, a longitudinal study by the National Child Development Study (NCDS), and also a survey by a MORI Poll in 1987, revealed that about 13 per cent of 23-year-old adults said that they had significant problems in literacy and numeracy. In terms of the general population this figure would be approximately six million people with literacy difficulties. Furthermore, of this group, there were 400,000 who reported that they could not read at all (Adult Literacy and Basic Skills Unit, 1988). The figures for difficulties in literacy and numeracy are higher – about 20 per cent – among long-term unemployed adults according to another survey conducted by the Manpower Services Commission in 1987. While these figures and the way they were obtained are open to discussion, they indicate a substantial problem in literacy and numeracy among the adult population in the UK. The figures include individuals who have general learning difficulties as well as those who have specific difficulties with language and literacy (Pumfrey and Reason 1991).

Some educationists (e.g. Pumfrey 1991) feel that all individuals, whether they have identified difficulties or otherwise, are capable of becoming literate, given thorough assessment and evaluation procedures and appropriate teaching and/or intervention. This is an optimistic view to take and one that we believe is sustainable, having considered the various aspects of literacy. In the same vein, others (e.g. Bradley and Bryant 1985) believe that pupils with literacy difficulties do not have qualitative differences from other pupils but quantitative. That is, their differences and difficulties are more substantial than most pupils' rather than being of a different nature.

The research literature in the field of literacy is extensive and we do not attempt to review it all here. In this chapter we focus on the interface between literacy and speech and language. We look at the developmental processes of reading, writing and spelling, ways of thinking about literacy, types of literacy difficulties which pupils display and the way these difficulties can be assessed and supported through teaching and intervention. An important difference between literacy and language is that language is acquired while literacy is taught. The implications are that difficulties in literacy may be due to factors within the individual, as well as due to factors in teaching reading, writing and spelling. In this chapter we look at both factors.

Development of Literacy Skills

This section considers the developmental processes and stages of reading, writing and spelling.

Reading

There are many models which illustrate the development of reading in children. The stages of reading presented here are based on evidence from research work with children by Chall (1983) and Harris and Coltheart (1986). Six main stages of reading development are identified by Chall from the earliest years up to adulthood while Harris and Coltheart look at the phases of development in the early years. Chall's model assumes that later development builds and expands on the earlier stages, that early skills will continue to develop and that the development of later stages does not rely necessarily on establishing earlier skills. Although stages are attributed to ages this varies in line with individual variation and across social and cultural groups. These stages reflect how children learn to read single words out loud through a variety of strategies until they become over-learned and automatic. Reading then becomes internalised and faster, extending to include a wider range of materials and then it becomes a means of accessing new knowledge.

In the final two stages of this model, reading is used to develop critical judgement about points of view and issues, and to appreciate different literary genres and authors and to challenge one's own belief systems. At this stage reading has become a tool for personal development. There is a claim that most of the adult population do not achieve the final two stages. One index is that tabloid newspapers have a target reading age of 12 years of age. We need to ask the question: what is our expectation for functional reading for pupils with literacy difficulties?

Chall's model

0-5 years	The pre-reading phase
5-7 years	Learning to read
7-9 years	Extending beginning reading
9-13 years	Reading to gain new understanding
13-18 years	Appreciation of evidence and arguments
18+ years	Construction and reconstruction of understandings

(from Pumfrey 1991: 97–8)

The *pre-reading stage* is the period when most spoken language acquisition takes place. Letters, words, phrases and sentences are recognised as representing speech, and labels and ideas connected with text are extended.

The *learning to read stage* is the phase when the child learns to associate letters and sounds and uses these skills to make meaning of written text. These basic skills become over-learned.

Harris and Coltheart (1986) look in detail at the first two stages and identify four phases within them: the sight-vocabulary phase, the discrimination-net phase; the phonological-recoding phase; and the orthographic phase.

The *sight-vocabulary phase* is the first identifiable phase of reading and occurs when the child has a small set of words, between ten and hundreds, which he or she can read aloud as sight vocabulary. Children as young as two years can be taught to do this (Fowler 1962) but the sight-vocabulary phase usually emerges at about four to five years of age. The child reads the words by the *direct procedure*, making no attempt to break down the words phonically. They seem to do more than simply recognise the words by their overall shape. They seem to be able to recognise letter strings although not making letter-sound associations. For example, they do not confuse letter strings and number strings; they recognise letters even when written in different sizes and cases within the same letter sequence and when the word shape has been radically altered; they reject strings of letters above eight showing an awareness of letter length in words.

The *discrimination-net phase* is when children read new words according to whether they think they already know how to read the word. That is, they match the new word against a familiar word from their sight vocabulary, using criteria such as word length, or a single letter or letter cluster. For example, *car* is read as *cat* and *robber* is read as *rabbit*. Children are aware that they are not able to read new words and making explicit familiar and new words is helpful to children in their mastery of new words. Many reading schemes do this. As children's discrimination net grows wider it becomes increasingly difficult for them to sustain this strategy for reading new words, which prompts them to develop a new strategy, phonological recoding.

The *phonological-recoding phase* marks the beginning of the use of letter-sound rules. That is, children start to use information about associating or mapping individual letters to individual sounds in order to read novel words. Children in this stage often sound out new words which is the hallmark of this phase. They are now able to attempt to read non-words, such as *dib* and *lub* because they are relying mainly on a phonics approach. Practitioners can obtain a great deal of information from matching the 'read' word to the 'target' word at this stage to find out how the children are mapping the letter-sound information.

This phase seems to offer the most obvious links between reading and speech. Children are mapping the printed word onto the image of how the word sounds, the word's *phonological (mental) representation*. The skills mentioned in the previous chapter, of perceiving rhyme and segmentation of sounds and syllables in words, are highly relevant to making the most of the phonological-recoding phase and the phonic approach to reading. Much research has been done on these aspects of phonological processing (e.g. Bradley and Bryant 1983; 1985) and strategies such as reading by analogy and rhyme have been identified (Goswami 1988). Analogy strategies help children read new words which share the same rhyme, that is the final VC (vowel-consonant) in a syllable, for instance, *m-eat* facilitates reading *s-eat, n-eat*. This research suggests that children will learn to read more successfully if, before learning to read, they appreciate 'that the spoken form of words can be broken down into sounds and that each sound can be represented by a letter' (that is recoded) (Harris and Coltheart 1986: 97). They are cracking the alphabetic code.

The *orthographic phase* emerges as children rely less on phonological recoding because they realise its shortcomings. It is inadequate for processing words which have different printed forms but the same phonological form, homophonic words, such as *flower/flour*, and for words which vary from the regular form, such as *ph* in *phone*, *gh* in *light* and *cough* and *tion* in *station*, that is, words which have exceptional spellings. Children gradually move from reading the word as it sounds and learn to read it as it is *spelled*. They move to a direct procedure for reading (see sight-vocabulary phase) which is like the adult form of reading and lends itself to increasing in speed and becoming internalised.

Literacy difficulties usually become apparent at the *alphabetic stage*, that is the phonological recoding phase in reading when letter-sound correspondences emerge and in writing when sound-grapheme correspondences emerge.

Writing

As early as possible children need to be aware that reading and writing are counterparts. The same prerequisites for reading obtain in that the children need to have an understanding of the symbolisation of text and the representation of the spoken form by the written form. Again, as with reading, children begin to write with the notion of the whole word and this can be encouraged when children do not know individual letter shapes.

Writing usually follows reading because of the development of hand-eye motor control, as well as letter formation and spelling which are dependent on knowing how to read.

Once children have developed sufficient hand-eye motor control to master holding a pencil and have started drawing, they usually begin the writing process. They usually begin by learning to write their name, starting with the most salient letter shapes, often the first letter. Letter formation needs to be taught and usually slows the process of writing, separating it in time from the development of reading. This separation may be temporarily bridged by using commercially published materials comprising printed words with which the child can form phrases and sentences. Thus, the child may learn to write single words as well as begin to write longer pieces of text. Methods such as *Breakthrough To Literacy* (Mackay *et al.* 1979) support this work.

Letter Formation

The formation of letters is the basis for writing words. Letter shape needs to be taught as a motor activity and kept separate from the speech sounds which they will come to represent for the child. In this respect, letter formation can be paralleled with babbling in speech development. The sounds which the infant produces cannot be imbued with meaning; it is a phase of motor development. One way of supporting meaning in the development of letter formation is through teaching methods which rely on cognitive strategies and mnemonics such as the programme, *Letterland* (Wendon 1984). In *Letterland* each letter is identified by a personality which has a name with the letter in the onset position, for example, 'w' is Water Witch, and 'g' is Golden Girl. Furthermore, the shape of the letter is fitted into the picture of the letter's identity. This allows for an easy step when the child is ready to segment the initial speech sound (phoneme) from the rest of the word and make letter-sound and sound-grapheme correspondences.

Often children will refer to the letter shape by its mnemonic name. Alternatively, the letter shapes can be referred to by their letter names, 'w' is called 'double u' and 's' is called 'es'. Practitioners may notice that pupils with substantial difficulties in phonological processing of sound-letter correspondences seem only to be able to refer to letters by their letter names and not by their sound; that is, 'c' is called 'see' and rarely 'kuh' by these children.

Most letters in written English are formed from circles, semicircles and straight vertical or horizontal lines. Hence, the child's perception of the orientation of a letter shape is important. Perceptual development is crucial and it is valuable to establish perceptual accuracy before moving on to writing the letters. This may help to limit letter-reversal confusions. Again, explicit verbalising of the motor movements involved, supports the motor activity.

Word shape can be learnt by the child by encouraging them to write the letters which they know and making some shape, such as a wiggly line, for the letters which they think might also be there but are unsure about. This helps children who have limited letter formation skills to formulate words by judging the number of (sounds) letter shapes they may have and going on to 'write' continuous text such as a longer phrase or sentence.

When children have a repertoire of sight vocabulary which they are beginning to analyse by phonological recoding and hence are beginning to form letter-sound correspondences, they are ready to recognise grapheme-sound correspondences and to start to write the words which are familiar to them.

Spelling

It is suggested that there are five stages which can be identified in the development of spelling: precommunicative, semiphonetic, phonetic, transitional and correct (Henderson 1985).

(1) *The precommunicative stage* is when the child's spelling may have one or two recognisable letter shapes but the word as a whole is not recognisable.

(2) *The semiphonetic stage* emerges as the child is able to form a recognisable word around a few letter shapes. All the sounds in the word may not be represented and there may be omitted letters, syllables and wiggly lines. There may be some influence from a visual image of the word. Most of the words attempted will be familiar from the child's sight vocabulary.

(3) *The phonetic stage* emerges around the time of the phonological recoding phase in reading. The child demonstrates spelling strategies based on the phonological representations of the word (Read 1986; Treiman 1993; Goswami 1992). Familiar developmental spellings at this stage are that the letter names of the vowels, such as *i* (aye) and *o* (ow), represent the vowel sound, such that TIM spells *time*, and ROT spells *wrote*. Pre-consonantal nasals are omitted, so that WIDO spells *window* and WET spells *went*. The morphological endings on words, such as the past tense and the comparative form *-er* are represented in their phonological form, so that DREST spells *dressed*, and HIY spells *higher*. Much letter formation at this stage is still formative and there are

a variety of reversal confusions displayed. For example, ONT (ont) spells *out*, DAD (dad) spells *bed*, HAB (hab) spells *had*, ZAY (zay) spells *say*.

(4) *The transition stage* shows that although there is still much phonetic influence on spelling there is evidence of the emergence of visually retained forms of the spelled form of the word. This is particularly shown in the spelling of exceptional word forms which are often the more frequently occurring words, such as *went, love, school, the*. Also there may be examples of partially recalled exceptional spellings such as the ch representing the 'kuh' sound, as in BRECHFUS as a spelling of *breakfast*. There may also be instances of inconsistency in the phonetic spelling, for instance, *friend/friends* may be spelled FRED and FRESSE, *went* spelled WET, WNT and WENT, within a few lines of each other.

(5) *The stage of correct spelling* emerges when the child shows the ability to spell and write consistently the adult conventional form of the word. It is worth remembering that when new or unfamiliar words are presented most individuals have recourse to a phonetic approach to spelling with possibly some influence from recalled visual representations of the word.

Ways of thinking about difficulties in literacy

There are different approaches to understanding difficulties in reading, writing and spelling which have grown from the professional fields involved in the area. There is no one agreed theoretical framework and three approaches are considered here: the medical approach, the psychoeducational and the cognitive neuropsychological.

A medical approach

For some time reading difficulties were thought to be caused by the lack of dominance of one of the two cerebral hemispheres (Orton 1925, 1926, 1937 cited in Pumfrey and Reason 1991). This theory is no longer supported by research findings. Associated theories which suggest that reading difficulties are due to mixed hand-eye laterality also remain unsubstantiated (Moseley 1988 cited in Pumfrey and Reason 1991). Other theories suggest that, although reading activity is most likely dependent on a functional interactive cognitive organisation, there seem to be localised areas of the brain primarily responsible for the performance of the whole system. Weaknesses in these areas, caused genetically, by a virus or by problems in late pregnancy, might give rise to reading difficulties. There is a growing body of interest in the effects of drugs and dietary biochemicals as a control or cure for reading difficulties. Nothing conclusive has emerged from research in this field.

Visual acuity is a natural area for concern in children who present with difficulties in reading and needs to be ruled out as a cause. Although children with reading difficulties may have faulty eye movements it is thought that these are most probably caused by the inability to phonologically process the text rather than any physical disability.

An educational approach

The issues which preoccupy educationists concern differentiating specific literacy difficulties from general learning difficulties which may affect children's reading. Identifying the nature of specific reading difficulties has implications for measuring its incidence, the provision of resources and the nature of teaching and intervention for children with these difficulties.

One of the key markers for differentiating between specific and general learning difficulties is the indication that in the case of specific literacy difficulties all other functioning is not giving rise to concern, particularly intellectual functioning. Yet, when the research literature is reviewed these assumptions may not be valid, suggesting that we need to look more closely at defining the specific nature of literacy difficulties (Stanovich 1994). More information is needed about the nature of these assumptions, by researching more the development of literacy among children who do not display reading difficulties, for comparison purposes.

Here are two case studies which throw light on the complexity of the relationship between dyslexia and intellectual functioning. Pollock (2001) gives a brief account of an eleven-year-old girl who was refused entry to secondary school because she was dyslexic and 'had a merely average IQ on the Weschler Intelligence Scale for Children (WISC III)' (p.171). Yet on a non-verbal intelligence assessment, the Raven's Coloured Matrices. she performed at the 95th percentile. When the head teacher was shown these results he accepted the girl into the school. Cooke (2002) discusses the case of a mature age student who entered university with almost no reading or writing skills. She could recognise very few words, she had difficulties spelling simple words and her handwriting was poor. She also had difficulties with numbers. Yet, she graduated successfully three years after entry. These studies serve to illustrate the complex relationship between dyslexia and intellectual functioning.

A cognitive (psycholinguistic) approach

The cognitive, or psycholinguistic, approach interprets literacy difficulties in terms of the underlying processing of language. The areas of language involved concern Form, primarily phonology and to a lesser extent grammar, which are the aspects of language least related to intellectual functioning, in contrast with semantic and pragmatic aspects (see Chapter 6).

Children seem to use processing strategies in developing their literacy to achieve a level of automatic functioning apparent in adult literacy. The key areas of cognitive functioning where weakness seems to bring about difficulties in learning literacy are phonological processing, working memory and accessing vocabulary. That is, if the child cannot access the word for spelling, reading or writing, or cannot manipulate the phonological representation, such as by segmentation, alliteration or rhyming or has difficulties with memory in processing these tasks, then literacy difficulties result. For example, *cat* is analogous to *hat* and *mat*, also found in *caterpillar* and has the same initial sound as *come*. Thus, children are segmenting words by sound and syllable, accessing phonologically similar words through rhyme and alliteration and using working memory to process these tasks.

Recent research in the area of speech difficulties (Stackhouse and Wells 1997) has developed a psycholinguistic framework which explains the relationship between speech and literacy difficulties. Subsequent research using this model demonstrates ways in which assessment, intervention and teaching can be planned and implemented to support children with speech and literacy difficulties (Stackhouse and Wells 2001).

Literacy difficulties

Throughout this chapter we refer to difficulties which pupils have with reading, writing and spelling as *literacy difficulties*. These difficulties are called *dyslexia*, which may refer in the narrow sense to reading difficulties only, while writing difficulties are called *dysgraphia*. There is a further term which refers to this cluster of difficulties, *specific learning difficulties* (SpLD). In a survey conducted on educational psychologists in 1989 the majority – 87 per cent – preferred the term 'specific learning difficulties' rather than dyslexia (Pumfrey and Reason 1991).

Dyslexia / Specific learning difficulties

Dyslexia is a combination of abilities and difficulties which affects learning processes in one or more areas of reading, spelling and writing and sometimes numeracy and language. A recent report described dyslexia as: 'when accurate and fluent word reading and/or spelling develops very incompletely or with great difficulty. This focuses on literacy learning at the "word level" and implies that the problem is severe and persistent despite appropriate learning opportunities' (cited in Cooke 2001: 48). Other areas affected may be speed of processing, short-term memory, sequencing, auditory and/or visual perception, spoken language and motor skills. Children with dyslexia may have normal intellectual abilities and come from a range of socio-economic and language backgrounds.

It is widely held that the core difficulty in dyslexia is the *phonological deficit hypothesis*. This hypothesis concerns poorly specified phonological representations (see previous chapter) which reflect higher level language difficulties rather than impairments in low level auditory mechanisms. Differences in performance of children with dyslexia are less likely due to sub-types of dyslexia as was previously thought (Pumfrey and Reason 1991). Variations in dyslexia are more likely due to the balance of strengths and difficulties in compensatory factors, such as visual memory, perceptual speed and print exposure. Better language skills is also a protective factor (Snowling 2001).

Other difficulties which may co-occur with dyslexia are attention deficit hyperactivity disorder (ADHD), high level social language difficulties (Asperger's syndrome) and motor coordination difficulties (dyspraxia). One study (Payton and Winfield 2000) reports that in a special school for pupils with dyslexia, 7 per cent of pupils had 'dyspraxia' noted in their statements and a further 32 per cent had references to fine motor coordination difficulties or major handwriting problems.

Difficulties with numeracy, *dyscalculia*, may co-occur with dyslexia, or may appear as a separate syndrome. The connection between mathematical difficulties and dyslexia has been largely overlooked. Students' failure to understand how the number system works or to appreciate place values may account for many mathematical difficulties experienced by dyslexic learners (Malmer 2000).

Humphrey (2002) argues that early identification of dsylexia offers children a good educational prognosis and the possibility of a more positive sense of self. Children might avoid the humiliation and trauma that they often experience prior to identification. Humphrey, in one study, found that most children had negative experiences at school prior to identification of dyslexia. Many of these experiences involved class teachers calling them stupid, lazy or slow. Pollock and Walker (1994) suggest that children will come to believe the negative images they are called. Humphrey proposes programmes which enhance self-concept and self-esteem for children with dyslexia. There are also implications for professional development for practitioners working with children in the early stages of learning to read.

Assessment

It is recommended that the assessment of children with reading difficulties should include information about

- their hearing and visual acuities;
- their previous learning as well as present progress;
- performance on assessments for reading difficulty;
- observations and interviews with the children, parents and the educational team involved.

This information needs to point up the children's strengths and weaknesses in literacy activities. There are roles for parents, teachers, psychologists and speech and language therapists in the accumulation of this information. For example, the class teacher is always involved in observing and gauging the pupils' responses to the nature and level of the tasks within the curriculum and amending the task where necessary. Support teachers, therapists and psychologists may be more involved in obtaining information from more formal assessment procedures. Parents' views about their child's progress need to be sought, particularly if special educational needs provision is being considered for the child.

The implications for interpreting literacy difficulties through the cognitive framework affect assessment, teaching and intervention. Assessment is usually task-specific, approaching the child's difficulty through phonological processing tasks rather than literacy ones and seeks to pinpoint the level of breakdown in processing. Intervention programmes are individual and aim to build up the processing strengths of the child, rather than focus on the obvious areas of difficulty. This is often done through raising the child's phonological awareness and there is a growing number of class-based teaching programmes for teachers to implement with pupils either before they embark on the process of learning literacy or to support specialised intervention programmes.

Teachers are often the first professionals to note that the pupil has difficulties approaching literacy tasks and would be the first source of referral to other more specialised agencies, such as psychology or medical, for further assessment for the pupil. Many local education authorities and schools have developed their own assessments for pupils with literacy difficulties and there are several commercially available procedures.

There is always a strong recommendation to identify pupils with literacy difficulties as early as possible in order to implement support and intervention programmes. Pre-literacy performance indicators are often employed because they have been shown to correlate highly with later literacy achievement. For example, the knowledge of letter names is one of the best predictors of later reading attainment, but teaching letter names will not guarantee successful reading. In other words, correlation, that is two factors which have a mutual relationship, does not indicate causality. Thus, the best that can happen using pre-literacy performance indicators is that some pupils 'at risk' may be identified. Alternatively, some pupils may be wrongly included and others wrongly excluded from the group thought to have potential literacy difficulties.

The range of assessments for evaluating literacy difficulties is extensive. The British Dyslexia Association recommends that there should be a screening procedure starting with a checklist completed by the class teacher on any pupil aged six whose developing literacy is a cause of concern. Further assessment includes ascertaining the child's cognitive profile, numeracy skills, auditory and visual sequencing, visual-motor skills and hand-eye coordination, phonological processing, comprehension of spoken and written language, expressive spoken language, reading and spelling strategies, and original writing. There should also be an appraisal of the pupil's social and emotional attitude to literacy.

Any assessment of a pupil with potential or actual literacy difficulties needs to include assessment of abilities and progress at a within-child, or intrapersonal, level as well as in comparison with peers for interpersonal comparison. Children learn literacy at different rates according to their abilities and appropriateness of teaching method. Practitioners involved in teaching literacy need to be aware of assessing and reflecting upon the efficacy of their own teaching methods and materials with their pupils.

Finally, practitioners are urged to appreciate 'the symbiotic relationship between assessment and teaching' (Pumfrey and Reason 1991: 27) when working with pupils who have literacy difficulties. There must be a constant and reciprocal relationship between the tasks which teachers and other practitioners offer these pupils, the pupils' response and performance, and subsequent tasks and teaching so that the assessment and teaching are continually informing each other.

Teaching and intervention

Pupils with literacy difficulties are not a homogeneous group and they display variation in reading performance and processes. There are four challenges to the practitioner: identifying the appropriate *method* for a particular *group* who are at a certain *stage* of development for a specific *aspect* of literacy. In other words, finding which aptitudes of the child interact most effectively with the teaching strategies. This is sometimes represented by 'aptitudes x interactions' (AIIs). Moreover, it is important to remember that most severe literacy difficulties are not likely to be 'cured'. Intervention and teaching seek to offer pupils strategies for managing literacy.

One approach to identifying effective AIIs is to develop individualised programmes for each pupil. Such programmes need to be closely monitored and amended in order to identify as precisely as possible their efficacy. Intervention and teaching programmes can adopt a cross-curricular approach to supporting pupils with literacy difficulties. For example, aspects of the intervention programme focusing on specific areas of processing weakness can be adapted for and supported in each curriculum subject; tapes and tape recorders can be provided for lengthy written work; provision of word processors and training in using them; provision of prepared worksheets, special vocabulary and notes. Again, close monitoring would identify which aspects were effective AIIs.

Where this is not possible, there are many specialised teaching approaches available to practitioners for pupils with literacy difficulties, such as *The Bangor Dyslexia Teaching System* (Miles 1989), *Children's Written Language Difficulties: Assessment and Management* (Snowling 1985), *Aston Index (Revised)* (Newton and Thomson 1982). There are also computer-assisted learning programmes for literacy difficulties. It is interesting to note that these programmes are based on principles and good practice for teaching literacy so that any and all pupils should benefit.

Additional teaching personnel provide in-class support, for example, to the class teacher through planning, or to pupils with literacy difficulties and facilitate their access to the curriculum. Classroom assistants can receive specialist training and qualifications to work with pupils with literacy difficulties (Layton and Deeny 1995). Where inclusive education is not available then teaching either by withdrawal or specialist classes may apply.

There is immense potential for inter-professional collaboration which would enhance the nature and quality of the management of literacy difficulties in this group of pupils. One initiative from the British Dyslexia Association is an early years training package, *Language and Literacy:*

joining together, developed by Wood *et al.* (2000) for multidisciplinary training courses for early years teachers, speech and language therapists and educational psychologists.

Linguistic minority pupils

Children who are literate in one language come to the second literacy with knowledge about the written form, and in this respect they could be advantaged rather than confused. Practitioners should consider how this prior knowledge could be developed by encouraging the transfer of skills, rather than ignoring the first literacy or seeing it as a disadvantage to the child's literacy development (Edwards 1995).

For pupils who are bilingual and have literacy difficulties there is a small but growing body of research on how they manage literacy in one or both languages. Studies of children whose literacies share a similar alphabet, such as English and Spanish, seem to rely on the literacy skills of the first learnt literacy to support the development of the second literacy (Durgunoglu *et al.* 1993). A recent conference and publication, *Multilingualism, Literacy and Dyslexia: a challenge for educators* (Peer and Reid 2000) and a review of the literature on literacy difficulties in bilingual children (Cline and Shamsi 2000) have contributed a great deal to the field. However, more studies are needed to investigate how bilingual children with phonological difficulties and literacy difficulties manage processing tasks involved in reading, writing and spelling.

Conclusion

The research on literacy difficulties is extensive and beyond the scope of this chapter, and we have focused on literacy difficulties as they relate to speech and language difficulties in the classroom. Within literacy we have included reading, writing and spelling, and we have looked at the development of all three aspects in some detail. We have pointed out that the cognitive framework is appropriate for understanding most aspects of literacy difficulty and associated speech and language processing difficulties. We have reviewed assessment procedures and teaching and intervention programmes. Early identification and intervention help children with literacy difficulties, whether severe and pervasive or less severe, to manage their difficulties, to succeed academically, and to develop a positive sense of self.

Further reading

Browne, A. (2001) *Developing Language and Literacy 3–8* (2nd edn). London: Paul Chapman.
Stackhouse, J. and Wells, B. (2001) *Children's Speech and Literacy Difficulties 2: identification and intervention*. London: Whurr.

Chapter 5

Difficulties formulating sentences

Introduction

In the first chapter, we presented one way of thinking about language in its interconnecting aspects of Form, Content and Use. In this chapter we consider the Form of language, specifically the form of words in utterances and sentences. We explore the nature of the form and structure of language, how it emerges in young children, continues to develop in young people, and the difficulties which some children display in formulating and constructing utterances. The developmental framework offers a way of appreciating the nature of difficulties in language structure which some children and young people display. There are also other ways of understanding the nature of language difficulties, such as the medical, linguistic and cognitive approaches, as we have seen in previous chapters. Language does not develop in a vacuum and its relationship with other factors, such as cognition and environmental factors, is considered.

Issues and procedures in assessment are discussed bearing in mind the range of differences in the heterogeneous group of children with language difficulties. Discussion of intervention and facilitating access to curriculum learning is informed by understanding the nature of the difficulties in formulating sentences.

Knowing about grammar

The continuing debate about whether, and how much, grammar should be overtly taught to pupils or whether it should be subsumed in the use and meaning of language does not concern us in this chapter. More interesting is that teachers' opinion seems to be divided about the nature and amount of information about linguistics that they need for working with children with expressive language difficulties. The majority feel that they need enough to be able to discuss with speech and language therapists and educational psychologists the detailed language assessments and intervention plans for the children they are involved with. A minority feel that they need to have basic skills in some aspects of the analysis of the child's language. These two attitudes may reflect the nature of teachers' needs and their differing levels of involvement in language support for children with language difficulties. Here, we offer a brief introduction to some of the terms and the parts of speech used in language description and analysis.

Describing grammar

According to the dictionary (Cobuild 1987): 'Grammar is the rules of a language, concerning the way in which you can put words together in order to make sentences.'

By looking at the patterns of combinations of words in spoken utterances, we are focusing on grammar, or syntax as it is also called. In Chapter 3 we saw that there are rules governing the way speech sound segments, segmental sequences and rhythm and stress are combined to make words. Linking words to form utterances is also governed by rules which show the relationship between words, and languages do it in different ways. 'Sentences are not simply random words strung together by means of various devices' (Aitchison 1999: 64). There are only a certain number of sentence patterns, which are identified by grammatical (syntactic) analysis.

Constituent analysis

Some words are clearly more closely related than others in the sentence and could be replaced by just one word. They form one component, or *constituent*. For example:

Mr Wormwood sold Miss Trunchbull an almost new car.[1]

Mr Wormwood	sold	Miss Trunchbull	an almost new car
He	sold	her	it

The constituents are identified as noun phrases (NP) and verb phrases (VP), as well as prepositional phrases (PP) and adverbial phrases AP.

Miss Trunchbull	had seen	the car	in the garage	yesterday
NP	VP	NP	PP	AP

Word combinations

Some important rules for combining words involve *word order, inflections* and *function words* (Aitchison 1999). Languages vary in their rules determining *word order*. English relies heavily on word order to make clear the meaning relationships in an utterance, for example:

That's the daughter of the man who owns Wormwood Motors in the village.

There is some flexibility about word order when words in constituents are kept together:

Nasty things, little girls are[1] = little girls are nasty things.

However, the meaning changes when the word order within constituents is changed:

Nasty girls are little things.

In other languages the verb may be placed first or last in the sentence. For instance, in Welsh, the appropriate sequence would be to place the verb first:

Wrote Mandy the story.

Alternatively, in Panjabi and Bengali the word order usually places the verb last:

Mandy the story wrote.

Bilingual speakers, occasionally, may carry over the word order from their first language into English, but this is generally not seen as a language difficulty and teaching can improve it.

Meaning relationship between words is shown through word endings, *inflections*. English is not a highly inflected language, but many languages have inflections which indicate the words which are together by sharing the same gender or number inflection.

Function words can also be used to indicate the meaning relation, such as *by, to, with, that, as, of*. For example:

The Trunchbull bullied Miss Honey.
Miss Honey was bullied *by* the Trunchbull.

The meaning in these two sentences is the same, although the word order is different. Function words, like *by*, help to maintain the meaning relation between the two people.

The importance of this brief overview of how we can describe grammar in sentences is that we use grammatical descriptions of sentences to identify difficulties in grammar. Some children have difficulties sequencing more than two or three constituents so that they function best when their utterances, and other people's are short and simple. They also have difficulties building up many words at phrase level so that they often only have one word in each phrase which also makes their sentences short. Their sentences may also be difficult to understand because word order is confused or necessary inflections and function words are missing.

Descriptive grammars

Descriptive grammars describe the patterns and word combinations which speakers actually use in their spoken language. These descriptions carry no notions of correctness or value judgements about incorrectness. They describe the rules which are in the speaker's language and consequently they can describe the range of variations to these rules.

In the arena of child language development, because descriptive grammars are able to describe the grammars of the individual speaker, they are the most sensitive means of describing the grammatical development of children's language. They provide a means for continuous description of the evolution of the child's language from its earliest beginnings towards the adult model. The grammar of the adult model may vary according to the speech community and the descriptive grammar can accommodate this as well. Using adult models of grammar, as a comparison to estimate the development of child language, could only provide negative information for most of the formative, and arguably the most interesting, period of language development in the child. For example, the grammar of a two-year-old child would be recorded as not having developed 'correct' plurals, tenses or pronouns and fail to identify that the child had acquired some rules and sequences for combining words and morphology. This approach is called an *error analysis* of child language. It can be effective when analysing more developed language which is nearer the adult target form, when it is important to identify parts of speech which are omitted or in the 'wrong' sequence.

In the field of speech and language difficulty, descriptive grammars have the power to describe the rules which individuals use in language in different contexts, and enable development and change to be noted.

The unit of analysis in spoken language

Spoken language does not have capital letters and full stops which indicate the beginning and end of sentences. Spoken language is not usually a continuous, seamless flow of grammatically correct elements punctuated in such a way that the listener knows the beginning and end of each sentence. Rather, it is usually a string of words, smoothly or hesitantly delivered and most often bounded by changes in intonation, pause, or by the next speaker taking their turn. Consequently, the term *utterance* is used to describe the unit for analysing grammar of spoken language. It is the unit, rather than 'sentence' used in studying child language development.

Child language development

For many people language development in children may seem to be an everyday miracle. However, it is a much studied area of language, mainly in English and less so in other languages. One of the most useful aspects of child language study for practitioners is *age/stage information* about language development. Relating important developmental stages to age offers a framework which can be used to compare development of children's language.

We often use the developmental sequence and pace shown by most children in their acquisition of language as a benchmark against which to measure the progress of children we suspect may have language difficulties. However, we need to have a critical eye when using developmental criteria, since 'preschool children vary extensively in the rate at which they develop language' (Richards 1994: 75). One study (Wells 1985) showed that in a group of children aged three and a half years the least advanced children had abilities similar to those of some children of two to two and a half years of age, while the most advanced children functioned at the level of some five-year-olds. Thus, the difference between the least and most advanced was between two and a half and three years. This is important when we make comparisons with the developmental spectrum. Consider which question we need to ask: how delayed does a child's language have to be in comparison with their chronological peers before we feel concerned about their language development? Or should our question be more concerned with the quality of the child's communication when we discuss language difficulty?

Earlier, we saw that meaning in utterances was structured by a limited number of patterns of word combinations, involving constituents and word order; making meaning at the level of words, was structured by inflections (e.g. word endings) and function words. The development of grammar in child language is usually described in terms of the growth of these features.

The development of the Form of language is usually described from pre-linguistic verbal 'noises' to complex and compound utterances, within the first five years of most children's lives. Children develop from 'making noises' to babbling, then using single word-like sequences of speech sounds which become established as words. They then begin to join words together into two-word utterances. This stage is usually recognised as the beginning of the child's awareness and knowledge that words have grammatical meaning. Typically, children progress through three-word utterances and then four-word utterances and finally usually after three years of age, they begin to develop complex multi-clause and multi-phrase utterances. They begin to use the structures of language to indicate statements, questions, probability, cause and effect, and verbal reasoning. Children who are deaf or severely hearing impaired develop through to the babbling stage and then stop. Some children, who are late to start to talk and progress slowly through the stages, are likely to be identified as having language difficulties.

There is a dramatic development of vocabulary (50–100 words) during the single word stage, as children learn to name objects, actions and attributes. Children with language difficulties may be reported as having had only limited vocabulary development in this period. Children's utterances show development of the combinations of constituents, phrases and the range of inflections and function words. For example:

> sock on, more milk, big ball, mummy bag, my turn
> daddy no gone, I wanna go,
> we go park now, I doing my car, dat car all broken

Beyond the four-word stage it is no longer helpful to describe grammatical development in utterances in terms of a word count. It is more useful to analyse the constituent relationships, NP, VP and AP, and the development of the phrase level structure.

Children using utterances with *complex* grammatical relations usually demonstrate well-developed meaning relations across all levels, at constituent, phrase and inflection and function word levels. There may still be some indications for further development, at word level, e.g. 'bestest'. For example:

> we was walking on the wall in the park with mummy's hand

However, utterances of children with grammatical difficulties often show development at constituent level, but limited grammatical feature development at phrase (e.g. adjectives, function words) and word level (inflections), so that their utterances sound 'telegrammatic' – with only the key information-carrying words.

The emergence of *compound* utterances is shown when children grammatically connect two ideas, because they are meaningfully related in some way, such as similarity, sequence, by contrast, or by cause and effect. For example:

My gran's old *and* she's clever.
We went swimming *and then* we had a pizza.
I kicked the ball *but* I didn't score a goal.
I like to read books *so* I can get a good job.
I was the prime suspect *because* of the Golden Syrup job.[1]

There are other ways of formulating compound sentences, such as by indicating a dependent relationship by embedding one sentence within another, often signalled by 'that ', 'which', 'what' clauses. For example:

I like the one *that* my Dad gave me for Christmas.
She was spiked and cut all over *when* she came out of the Chokey.
Tell me *what* you think of my chocolate cake.
She didn't want to put them off *before* they started.

Some children who can formulate simple sentences have difficulties formulating compound sentences. There may be several explanations for this. Children with language difficulties may have limited auditory sequential memory abilities and be unable to manage long strings of word sequences. They may also have difficulties managing the grammatical relationships involved in connecting the ideas because they are hierarchical, embedded, dependent or causal.

At the same time as constituent and phrase level grammar is developing, so are the grammatical structures which shape word level relationships in utterances. Words, function words and inflections are known as **morphemes** and are referred to by the term **morphology**. Morphemes which exist as words in their own right are called free morphemes; e.g. *cup, give, car* as well as function words, e.g. *by, from, in, under, to, at, the.* Other morphemes only occur attached to words, for example *-ly*, as in *quickly, gently*, and *-ing*, as in *going, running.* These are called bound morphemes. They are obligatory in English for grammatical utterances.

Brown's work (1973) and that of others (e.g. de Villiers and de Villiers 1973) who studied child language development identifies a group of morphemes which emerge early in syntactic development. These fourteen words and word endings include:

-ing   : as in *shouting*
-ed   : as in *opened*
- 's   : as in *mummy's*
-a/the : as in *a dog, the car*
- s   : as in *she wins*
- is/are: as in *she is playing, they are reading*

These early studies show that children are learning function words and inflections which have little or no meaning in themselves, in order to indicate grammatical change, such as present or past tenses, singular and plural.

Further research conducted in the 1970s (Dulay and Burt 1977) shows that children who are acquiring English as a second language also seem to acquire these morphemes early in their development of English. Moreover, it seems that this is the case whatever the mother tongue of the child (Fathman 1975).

Brown's (1973) findings suggest that there is an order of morpheme acquisition, that is, some morphemes emerge earlier than others in language development of children. Other research (Nelson 1981) indicates that some children are likely to acquire these morphemes idiosyncratically. Usually most children have acquired many of these early emerging morphemes by two and a half years of age (Wells 1985).

A frequent way of assessing children's early language development is to measure their grammar development by calculating the average number of morphemes used in utterances, so-called Mean Length of Utterance (MLU). From a sample of a child's spontaneous language, the morphemes in each utterances are counted. For example:

Daddy	bring	me	choo-choo	=	4	morphemes
1	2	3	4			
Mummy	eat – ed	a	sandwich	=	5	morphemes
1	2 3	4	5			
Doggie	's	bed	broke	=	4	morphemes
1	2	3	4			
I	gotta	go		=	3	morphemes
1	2	3				

Divide the total number of morphemes by the total number of utterances to give the mean length of utterance or MLU: 16/4 = 4

According to Brown an MLU of 4 would be about right for a child aged 3;6–4years.

Other information relating MLU to age: 1 MLU: 18 months
                                        2 MLU: 24 months
                                        3 MLU: 30 months

Children who have difficulties developing grammar often show a lack of, or only limited, morpheme development which may remain undeveloped until intervention. It is often difficult to successfully teach morphemes because of their limited meaning.

Most grammatical structures are in place by the age of five years. However, there is evidence (e.g. Carol Chomsky 1969; Perera 1986) that children continue to acquire more complex forms and rules of grammar up to ten years of age and beyond. One of the most common ways for them to develop further grammatical structures is through reading and writing.

Characteristics of children with difficulties formulating sentences

While children with specific language difficulties are a heterogeneous group, there are characteristics in language and learning behaviour which many of them share. One of the central characteristics is that they have cognitive abilities in line with their peers, with a significant discrepancy between their language age and their chronological and mental ability age (Conti-Ramsden and Botting 1999).

Some children have difficulties combining more than two or three constituents or building up words at phrase level, so that their sentences are usually short and simple. They usually have difficulties attempting longer utterances and joining two ideas together using conjunctions (complex utterances). These difficulties will also affect reading and writing. In addition many children with specific difficulties in language also have difficulties with related cognitive functions, particularly auditory memory and auditory sequencing. They often have difficulties understanding some sentence structures.

It remains difficult to differentiate in the early years between those language difficulties which will resolve on their own, those which will resolve with support and intervention and those which remain with the individual. About 60 per cent of children who have preschool language difficulties go on to have persistent language difficulties in formulating utterances and they are referred to as having *specific language impairment (SLI)* or *specific speech and language needs (SSLN)* (Dockrell and Lindsay 1998). There is an increasing body of experimental and longitudinal case study information which aims to provide more reliable ways of identifying and distinguishing between transient and pervasive language difficulties. While information about language processing in children and young people with persisting SSLN increases understanding about their unique language development, more information is needed about the way these children learn.

There is a small group of children who following damage to the brain in childhood, may have language difficulties. They usually recover their language skills over a period of a few years and often with support and intervention from therapists and teachers. They may follow a pattern of development in recovery which is slightly different from their first developmental patterns. In some ways it may appear to be similar to certain aspects of adult language loss and recovery.

Associated factors

The most frequently identified factors associated with language difficulty are:

- global learning difficulties
- hearing impairment
- poverty (economic disadvantage)

Language difficulty is *secondary* to these primary difficulties. Intervention and support focused on language and communication needs to take account of the primary difficulty. Intervention and support should be included in a more comprehensive approach to meeting the child's needs rather than happening in isolation.

In children with certain severe forms of slow learning syndromes not all aspects of language are affected. Aspects of Form, such as grammar, are often not affected because they are least associated with cognitive development. Many children with learning difficulties develop aspects of Form satisfactorily.

Children with hearing impairment usually need to be taught oral or/and sign language. Some sign languages only have grammatical structure at constituent and word order level (e.g. British Sign Language, Makaton) while others reflect the phrase and word level grammatical structures of spoken language (e.g. Paget-Gorman Signing System). Some children with hearing impairment demonstrate additional difficulties developing grammatical structures.

Research evidence supports strong links between language delay and poverty. In a recent study, more than half of the preschool children studied, from disadvantaged socio-economic backgrounds, were found to be language-delayed. Girls' receptive language abilities were significantly better than boys' and all participants' language skills were significantly lower than their cognitive abilities (Locke *et al.* 2002). In severe cases of social deprivation, such as maternal deprivation, or depression in the main caregiver, children's language development may be delayed. There may be additional difficulties since children in these situations are also more likely to be prone to illness and poor nutrition (Townsend and Davidson 1982). Language delay for these reasons is likely to have long-term implications for language abilities in adolescence and adulthood.

Memory, sequencing and organisational skills

Pupils with language difficulties may also have difficulties with memory and in particular short-term memory which may be the cause of difficulty formulating sentences. However, children may have satisfactory short-term memories and still have difficulties formulating sentences. In these cases it seems more likely that they have difficulties managing the hierarchical nature of grammatical structures (Cromer 1991). That is, they have difficulties understanding and using sentences with internal structures which have dependent or embedded elements (described earlier). It may be difficult to distinguish between children with memory and/or hierarchy difficulties because they produce similar responses. In the following sentence, they are likely to think that the Pied Piper drowned, not the rats.

The rats who followed the Pied Piper drowned in the river

Many children with specific language difficulties have memory and organisational difficulties pervading all aspects of their everyday lives. They may have difficulty remembering to do homework and bring it into school, completing errands, prioritising tasks, or organising or packing their school/PE bag. It may also be seen in other areas of curriculum learning, such as mathematics and science. This difficulty may also extend into understanding and organising time and space. They may have difficulty estimating distance or travelling time, recounting or organising events of their day; and interpreting clock and calendar time. Curriculum subjects such as history and geography may present a considerable challenge.

Ways of thinking about expressive language difficulties

In previous chapters we have discussed understanding the nature and causes of speech and language difficulties in a variety of approaches. There are medical, linguistic, cognitive and educational ways of understanding difficulties in formulating utterances.

A medical approach

A medical approach to understanding grammatical difficulties in expressive spoken language looks for genetic, neurological and physical explanations. Studies of family histories suggest that for a small group of children there may be a hereditary link, stronger through the male line, and that some *specific language impairments (SLI)* may be autosomally genetically linked (Pembrey 1992). In other cases, children with this type of difficulty may have some neurological weakness, possibly through slow brain maturation, lack of cerebral hemisphere dominance or through trauma at birth. So-called 'clumsy' children may show language difficulties because of neurological weakness. Children and young people may display language difficulties caused by brain damage due to accidents or viral infections such as meningitis. The resulting language difficulty is usually severe and may be called *childhood aphasia* or *acquired childhood language impairment*. In some cases, children may also show other difficulties, such as with speech, which is another aspect of the Form of language.

The medical approach offers valuable insights into the cause of some expressive language difficulties and in some cases offers an explanation, through genetic links, for the association between language difficulty and other difficulties, such as severe learning difficulties. However, we must look to other approaches for understanding language difficulty and how we might support the learning of children with such difficulties.

A linguistic approach

A linguistic approach to understanding grammatical difficulties offers important perspectives:

1. It offers a description of children's language and language development which allows comparisons with typical development.
2. A detailed description of the different aspects of grammatical

development gives a profile of constituent, phrase and word level grammar which can inform assessment and identification of areas of difficulty and guide planning support and intervention.

A strength of the linguistic perspective is that it offers a description of a child's atypical language which can be set within a context of the developmental spectrum, whether this is in comparison with peers or within the child's own developmental profile.

A linguistic approach gives a perspective across different aspects of language, based on the Bloom and Lahey (1978) model. Difficulties in discrete categories of language can be identified as well as difficulties which overlap language categories. For example, within the category of Form, children with grammatical difficulties can also have difficulties with phonology, while a recent study shows that children with grammatical difficulties may also have sociability difficulties in communicating (Donlan and Masters 2000). The model of language categories usually applies to expressive language. Yet, often children with grammatical difficulties have difficulties comprehending grammatical structures they have not acquired. (See Chapter 8).

A linguistic perspective offers an explanation of the controversy surrounding children's difficulties formulating sentences. Two frequently occurring difficulties shown by these children are in distinguishing the roles of verbs and nouns, and using verbs in appropriate structures. For example:

a) *the duck scruts flowers*: difficulty in knowing that *scruts* is a verb
b) *I'll give you*: difficulty in recognising that this structure is incomplete, because *give* must have two object noun phrases: *I'll give **you a hug***

One explanation is that these children may not have the linguistic knowledge to recognise grammatical roles of words; for example, between nouns and verbs, or recognise and use the appropriate structures for verbs (van der Lely 1994). A more cognitive (psycholinguistic) explanation is that they have processing problems related to working memory. They show grammatical difficulties because there is too much processing demanded to make sentence structures with unfamilar words, or to use two noun phrases with a verb (O'Hara and Johnston 1997).

A cognitive (psycholinguistic) approach

A cognitive psycholinguistic approach looks at language processing and offers three valuable perspectives:

1. a model of language processing, closely related to other cognitive functions which explains language difficulties in terms of limits in cognitive functions;
2. a comparison of verbal performance with non-verbal performance to identify discrepancies between specific language difficulties and more global learning difficulties;
3. a strong framework for identification ('diagnosis') and assessment of difficulties, and indicators for intervention.

A framework for assessment is one of the strengths of the cognitive approach. Children with difficulties formulating utterances often have poor auditory memory abilities, sequencing difficulties, selective attention difficulties as well as displaying difficulties in reading and writing. Assessing these functions can reveal a profile of abilities which may inform support or intervention based on strengthening cognitive functions, as well as working directly on aspects of grammatical development.

However, an important weakness of all these models is that they offer few insights for supporting learning in the curriculum for children with grammatical difficulties.

An educational approach

An educational approach to children with grammar difficulties offers perspectives which inform the teaching and learning environment:

1. to understand how grammatical difficulties (receptive and expressive) impact on the academic and social learning of the child, within and beyond school;
2. to use approaches to teaching and learning which seek to support difficulties in grammar in order to enable learning;
3. to interpret information from linguistic and cognitive approaches in planning and evaluating teaching and learning.

The educational implications for linguistic and cognitive perspectives of grammatical difficulties are that consideration of grammatical structures in language demands will heavily influence teaching and learning the curriculum. In particular, children with these difficulties need to be exposed to new words and their grammatical roles in a planned and systematic way. More pervasively, there are implications for the length and complexity of giving or following instructions, for participating in classroom or small group discussion, as well as learning through reading and writing.

Assessment

Assessment information which is helpful to identifying the nature and severity of children's needs and informs provision and teaching must comprise standardised testing and systematic observation. While there are a variety of procedures to help the practitioner assess difficulties in formulating sentences, it is important to bear in mind that 'assessment must be developmentally and culturally appropriate, taking into account the cognitive and social aspects of development.' (Dockrell and Messer 1999: 124).

The class teacher and support teacher may wish to assess a child's language skills to inform their concerns, and with a view to referring the pupil to a colleague, such as a speech and language therapist or an educational psychologist, for more in-depth assessment. This kind of assessment, a *screening* procedure, needs to be feasible in the classroom with an individual child or with a small group. Initial screening procedures for pupils with language difficulties are often *checklists* which check, through teacher observation, pupils' speech sounds and sentence formulation. One checklist in the UK is available from the Association for All Speech Impaired Children (AFASIC 1991) and an example from it can be found at the end of the chapter. Checklists are based on developmental age/stage information and offer criteria for comparing a child's development with that of peers.

There are other screening procedures which offer more detailed information concerning pupils' language structures, often entailing some interaction to elicit sentences, and based on age/stage information. An example from the UK is the *Derbyshire Rapid Screening Test* (Knowles and Masidlover 1982). It is designed for use with children with suspected language difficulties in the context of moderate global learning difficulties. There is another assessment procedure which has 'screening' in its title, the *Language Assessment, Remediation and Screening Procedure* (LARSP) (Crystal *et al.* 1976). It is, in fact, a detailed linguistic analysis of an individual's utterances which can be quite lengthy and is usually done by speech and language therapists, although some teachers working closely with therapists use it confidently.

Following the screening procedure which is the first step to ascertain whether a difficulty exists, the main purposes of further assessment of language difficulties are:

1. to identify what aspect(s) of language is effected;
2. to identify extent of the difficulty;
3. to indicate possible goals for support and intervention;
4. to measure change in the difficulty over time with or without support and intervention.

Assessments which give more information about grammatical abilities are standardised on peer populations in the UK; for example the *Reynell Developmental Language Scales* (RDLS) (expressive and receptive scales) (Edwards *et al.* 1997); the *Bus Story* (Renfrew 1972); and for understanding grammatical structures, the *Test for the Reception of Grammar* (TROG) (Bishop 1989). However, these tests need to be individually administered usually by a specialist practitioner. While it may be tempting to rely on standardised test results, research shows that there are variations in scores across tests on children who do not have difficulties. On some tests the scores were age-appropriate and on others they were below their age (Howlin and Cross 1994 cited in Dockrell and Messer 1999). Furthermore, one-off assessment procedures are of limited value unless they are considered together with information gathered on a day-to-day basis.

Systematic observations offer insights about children's communicative abilities and difficulties as they attempt daily classroom activities and learning tasks. Information over time informs practitioners' knowledge about the child's way of learning and learning needs. This approach to assessment of pupils' language difficulties leads to collaboration between practitioners working in the classroom and those who work beyond.

Support and intervention

Drawing on the knowledge and theoretical perspectives presented in the chapter, there are two principles which underpin support and intervention for children with language difficulties: ensuring understanding, and optimising meaningful communication. A further important orientation is to work around the developmental continuum although this may not always be appropriate for the child's language development. Children with SSLN have cognitive abilities in line with those of their peers, and can potentially learn the curriculum if their language needs are appropriately supported

Implementing strategies with children who have language difficulties can help their language development and their learning. However, though strategies are useful tools they need to be discarded when they have fulfilled their purpose and the learner no longer relies on them for support.

Promoting understanding can be done in a variety of ways. The most important way is for teachers and other practitioners to be aware of the level of complexity of their own language to the children. Effective strategies include:

- using shorter utterances, expressing one key piece of information at a time;
- ensuring attention and listening by using the learner's name;
- developing class rules and signals to facilitate listening;
- using tape recorders/headphones to replay auditory material such as instructions;
- using visual material which supports auditory information, particularly key visuals which interpret the learning aim of the session;
- offering grammatically accurate modelled versions of children's responses;
- extending their responses to include other relevant, meaningful information.

Reading and written work in curriculum areas can be differentiated to support children with grammatical difficulties. Modelling can be done in written work, through worksheets; for example, a complete model sentence frame about the topic can be followed by sentences about different aspects of the topic, which have parts of them missing, such as the names of cities, dates, or types of weather. On other occasions this strategy can be used to support learning of particular aspects of grammar, such as prepositions, which have been identified in the child's individual education plan (IEP) following assessment.

Strategies which involve group work emphasise communication and help develop confidence in speaking in children with language difficulties. Activities need to be carefully planned in terms of targeted structures, level of comprehension and pairing/grouping of children. Books, such as *Grammar Fames and Activities 1* (Watcyn-Jones and Howard-Williams 2001), although originally aimed at teaching students of English, are useful resources.

Conclusion

Children with difficulties formulating sentences are a heterogeneous group. Each individual is unique in her/his difficulties because of the cause and nature of the difficulty, different experiences at home and at school and different learning patterns. These children have specific language difficulties with learning abilities in line with their peers. Medical, linguistic, cognitive and educational perspectives contribute to understanding difficulties with grammar and identifying appropriate assessment and intervention strategies. Support and intervention in the classroom through strategies ensuring understanding and promoting communication can help children with difficulties in grammar to access the curriculum. Difficulties in aspects of Form also influence meaning in language, which is the topic of the next chapter.

[1] From *Mathilda* by Roald Dahl.

Further reading

Dockrell, J. and Messer, D. (1999) *Children's Language and Communication Difficulties*. London: Cassell.

The AFASIC checklists

An example page from the speech and language screening test for 6- to 10-year-olds

4 Errors in sound

a) Omits the beginnings and endings of words e.g. 'pretending' becomes 'tending'   [ ]
b) Reduces multisyllabic words e.g. 'potato' becomes 'tato'   [ ]
c) Speaks less intelligibly when excited   [ ]
d) Speaks less intelligibly when attempting a lengthy utterance   [ ]
e) Shows persistent confusion between voiced and unvoiced sounds
   e.g. p/b, f/v, t/d, k/g   [ ]

TOTAL FOR THIS SECTION

5 Communication

a) Has delayed understanding of question words e.g. what, who   [ ]
b) Does not follow instructions without prompting   [ ]
c) Offers limited verbal comments on own activities   [ ]
d) Shows unexpected responses to questions   [ ]
e) Uses inappropriate intonation and volume when speaking   [ ]

TOTAL FOR THIS SECTION

6 Play and recreation

a) Has difficulty following a story without many cues   [ ]
b) Has no play involving sounds, rhymes or words   [ ]
c) Is slow to learn rules of group games and position in sports   [ ]
d) Enjoys the visual content of television programmes but finds it hard
    to follow stories and plots   [ ]
e) Humour tends towards visual and slapstick with poor appreciation of
    verbal jokes and puns   [ ]

TOTAL FOR THIS SECTION

Chapter 6

Difficulties with meaning in language

Introduction

This chapter deals with exploring the development of, and difficulties in, meaning in language. Meaning in language is also called **semantics,** and **Content** in Bloom and Lahey's terms. It develops through organisation of linguistic information, such as words, and is also informed by our cognition, conceptual knowledge of the world and the context of the language. The relationship between meaning in language, context and conceptual development is intimate and complex and we will explore aspects of this relationship.

As in previous chapters, we take a developmental approach to understanding difficulties in expressing meaning and we discuss the development of meaning as it seems to occur in most children. We consider other perspectives, namely linguistic and neuropsychological, for describing meaning in language, the processing mechanisms of storing, accessing and retrieving meaning, and the difficulties which some pupils show in this aspect of language. We evaluate how they can contribute to assessing difficulties of meaning in language and supporting and intervening with children who have these difficulties.

What is a word? Defining terms

There is some debate about the identity of the 'word' (also called vocabulary, lexis and lexicon). For example, would *cat* and *cats* be recognised as being the same word? Would *put on*, meaning *wear*, be recognised as one or two words? Would the phrase *kick the bucket*, meaning *die*, be one word? This kind of debate has led some linguists to use the term **lexeme** which includes the different instances of the word, counting them as 'the same' lexeme. This embraces multi-word lexemes which have one meaning, such as *put on* or *kick the bucket* (Crystal 1981). This issue is important for learners who have difficulties with meaning. When we are assessing vocabulary, one approach is counting the number of words or lexemes pupils have in their expressive vocabularies. However, a word count as a measure of expressive language ability is controversial. Word counts are often used in the very early stages of monitoring the development of language in young as well as in older individuals who have little speech. It is worth considering how much language information is left unanalysed after a word count. Word counts tell us nothing about the nature, roles and relations of the words used, such as the meanings or grammatical functions the words have adopted in the utterance.

Despite these caveats, vocabulary size is a powerful measure used in national surveys. For example, in the United States the Harvard Language Study informs us that 'children of poverty' enter formal school settings with a vocabulary that is less than half the size of the average, non-poverty child. Children of professional families start school with an average vocabulary of 5,000 words whereas children of poverty have average vocabularies of 2,000 words (Garcia 2001). The survey draws out the implications for literacy development and academic achievement for disadvantaged children of poverty. However, practitioners and researchers need to distinguish between disadvantage, 'deficit' and learning need and to bear in mind that vocabulary size is only part of language and learning. Nevertheless, there are implications for teaching and learning of vocabulary.

What's in a word?

When children come to learn words they are faced with three main tasks: to develop words as labels, packages and networks (Aitchison 1994). Firstly, the word, or lexeme, is a *label* or the linguistic referent for an object, person, attribute or action in the outside world. Secondly, it carries a *package* of information about conceptual meaning which gradually becomes more complex and refined as the child's conceptual development progresses. Also, in this package is information about the word's grammatical role (sometimes called thematic role) in a sentence or utterance, such as being a noun or a verb, or the actor or receiver of an action. Thirdly, the lexeme operates within a *network* of how it relates to other words, for example by meaning the same, or opposite, or by being in the same category. As children develop words they face all these tasks at the same time and when there are difficulties in any of these tasks then meaning in language is affected.

Finally, as we have discussed in previous chapters, the lexeme also carries information about speech sounds, syllable sequences and morphology, which are sometimes referred to as the 'internal architecture' of the word.

Let us consider first the labelling task facing children.

The labelling task

The labelling task is a process of symbolisation for the child, when the realisation occurs that the auditory signal means or refers to an object, person, activity or attribute. For an infant this task usually goes on between the child and the parents or caregiver, possibly in a very tutorial way. 'What's this?' asks the adult. 'It's a car. Brrmmm', continues the adult. Most children exposed to this tutorship commence their acquisition of words. They learn that everything has a lexical referent. This may become evident in some preschool children, aged three to five years, when they continually ask the names of objects, and parts of objects. Children are not passive recipients of words but interactive.

Compare this method of learning vocabulary with how new words are introduced and taught in the nursery or classroom. Consider how you would introduce new vocabulary to pupils. Most school-aged children do not need the intensive one-to-one 'tutoring' when learning new words but some will if they are to acquire new vocabulary consistently.

Difficulties learning to label

For this early stage of learning words, children not only need supportive environments, they also need to be ready to acquire this level of symbolisation. It seems that their physical and cognitive maturation needs to be at a stage when they can focus on and be attentive to the object or activity being labelled. They need to have developed the notion of object permanence and levels of symbolisation in pictures and in play objects. It is thought that the necessary auditory and linguistic symbolisation develops from these achievements (Bloom 1973).

Strategies to support the child's learning to label depend to some extent on the factors causing the difficulty. Some children, often with associated physical and learning difficulties, may not acquire these physical and cognitive skills and consequently have difficulty learning verbal labels. They have difficulties storing the auditory information. To support these children an effective strategy seems to be to develop labelling through gesture and systems such as Makaton signing (Walker 1978; Walker and Armfield 1981) which are very successful. Makaton offers the child a gestural level of language symbolisation which can be developed and linked with speech. Some children may respond to printed word labels. For other children, who show difficulty with symbolising in any form, the approach must be to develop symbolisation through play, pictures and, later, environmental sounds, before embarking on linguistic symbols such as gestures.

Some children who seem to be able to symbolise through play and visual performance, such as drawing, may have a specific difficulty making sense of, and storing, auditory information and thus difficulty in learning words. It is often problematic getting a consistent audiometry result for these children. Children with this difficulty may be referred to as having *central auditory perception* difficulties or *auditory verbal agnosia*. Case studies of such children show that it is unlikely that they will acquire verbal labels and their spoken language is limited (Adams *et al.* 1997). One recent case study showed that a successful strategy used gesture and visual symbolisation; the child began to learn words through picture matching, printed labels and through Makaton (Martin and Reilly 1995).

By contrast, for many children who have hearing impairments, auditory support such as a hearing aid, a classroom loop system or lip-reading together with appropriate adult interaction may be sufficient in helping them to acquire words because their ability to process language and to make linguistic reference is intact.

One of the more frequently used approaches to assessment of labelling skills is by *confrontation naming tasks*, asking the child or young person to name the picture, object or activity pointed to by the assessor. While having the merits of a simple and straightforward approach, this method of assessment has several drawbacks. Picture naming may depend on a level of perceptual ability beyond the child, although he or she may know the word; it is a contrived and decontextualised way of looking at vocabulary, and most important, it is a potentially hostile interaction in which some children may perform adversely.

The packaging task

Children usually learn a word initially in the context of one referent; *dog* refers to the one dog they first learn to label. Children are then faced with the task of learning that the word *dog* refers to a wider range of referents, in this case, all dogs, and that it does not refer to other smallish furry four-legged animals. The limited reference of a word shows that the child has an underextended meaning of the word. *Underextension* is very common in vocabulary development in children who are developing vocabulary both with and without difficulties. The child discussed by Martin and Reilly (1995), who had substantial difficulties acquiring words and their referents, displayed considerable difficulty extending the use of the word *dog* from a familiar single referent, which was one familiar picture of a dog, to other pictures of different dogs. He showed a conceptual rigidity through underextending the reference of the word meaning. In the same way, in classrooms underextended meaning may show itself by children not appreciating the conceptual reference of words.

By contrast, children can use words by *overextending* the range of reference, including referents which would be excluded by older children and adults. For example, the word 'daddy' referring to all men, or 'moon' referring to moon, cow's horns, and a round lemon slice (Bowerman 1980). Overextension is a much less common feature of developing vocabulary yet more complex and it may be due to various factors, such as limited experience, pronunciation difficulties and idiosyncratic perceptions.

As children's perception develops and they begin to focus on the characteristics which adults are aware of, they learn to differentiate meanings and words more and to package meanings of words in a similar way to the adults in their speech community. However, some children have difficulty doing this. They continue to package the meaning of their words according to their own analysis and perception of salience so that their use of words appears overextended or idiosyncratic in comparison with an adult's. Simply introducing new words to these children may not be successful because it assumes that the child shares the adult package of word meaning about the object or action and only lacks the new label. We need to identify what these children perceive about the object, which might be its shape, colour, use, in order to understand how they have packaged the meaning of words they use.

We know from studies with adults on semantic memory and word associations that words can be retrieved and stored by accessing other information, through meaning associations. It is the development of organisation of the lexicon by association of meaning to which we now turn.

Network building: a system of contrasts

Lexemes can be organised by the way their meanings relate to each other, such as by sameness or oppositeness, by category and by surface form similarities.

Lexemes which are related by similar meaning are called *synonyms*, such as *couch/sofa/settee*, *sad/unhappy/depressed*, *book/volume/paperback*. Children with word difficulties may retrieve a synonym of the target word, such as *colours* for *paints* and while acceptable, it can impede effective under-standing and lead to communication breakdown.

There are groups of words which are related by opposite meanings, *antonyms*, such as *more/less*, *little/big*, *old/young*. There are several possible explanations for confusion in understanding and using these words. Many of the meanings of these words are relative; that is, a baby is 'little' in comparison with an adult, but 'big' in comparison with a doll. Also there is a nearness of meaning between polar opposite words because they share the same features of meaning, except for one. For example, *push* and *pull* share several semantic features with only one distinguishing feature, direction. This is likely to cause confusion as with this five-year-old child, who has language difficulties, describing a picture to an adult (taken from Crystal 1983):

> Child: then look. catch the fish/and then pushed it in
> Adult: that's right/he caught the fish/and the fish pulled him in

There are implications for teaching opposites and it is advisable to avoid decontextualised teaching through flash cards where the salience of the single distinguishing feature may not be evident.

Very young children often reverse personal pronouns so that 'I' and 'you' are confused as when *You broke it* means *I broke it*; and children may also confuse the gender referent for third person personal pronouns, 'he' and 'she'. These confusions have been noted as persistent features in the language of older children with severe semantic difficulties and who may have autistic tendencies.

There are words which are related because they refer to the same category or semantic field. For example, words such as *cupboard, table, TV,* are members of the category *furniture,* that is they are **subordinates** of a **superordinate** category of words. Other category words are *fruit, flowers, transport, animals, people.* Developmentally, children tend to learn first the names of members of the category and later they learn the category word. A three-year-old child may know the words *apple, orange, banana* but not relate them to the word *fruit.* An example from Macnamara (1982) documents a child refusing to accept that a *horse* was also an *animal,* possibly because he was operating on a strategy of 'one object – one name'. Yet young children seem to have no problem in referring to a miscellaneous group of animals as *animals* or to an assortment of playthings as *toys.* Some children and young people have difficulties relating words to semantic fields and respecting concept boundaries. Thus, they may include words in a semantic field from a related category, such as including vegetable words with fruit words, *banana, apple, cabbage, pear* (Landells 1989).

Words may also be related **serially,** such as numbers, months of the year, days of the week, and less frequently they may be related through **incompatibility,** such as colour words.

Finally, there are words which are not related through meaning but through their surface forms which either sound the same – **homonyms**, such as *flour/flower, meat/meet, red/read* – or look the same in the written form – **homographs**, such as *lead/lead, object/object*. These words are often the focus of literacy work rather than work on meaning. From a different perspective, there are words which have multiple meanings and this is called **polysemy**. For example, *summit* has two meanings: (i) top of a mountain and (ii) an important international meeting. This is an important feature of meaning in language which pupils often have difficulties with and we discuss it further.

Polysemy: one lexeme – different meanings

The important point about understanding **polysemy** is that the meaning of words is constituted by the context in which they occur. For example, if talk is about *climbers* and *mountains*, by networking associations we can work out that the appropriate meaning of *summit* is 'mountain top' rather than 'international meeting'. Most children learn polysemy without much difficulty. However, children with difficulties learning words and meaning show difficulty learning more than one meaning for a word. They seem to follow the strategy: one referent – one word.

Children learn the different meanings of polysemous words as they occur in different contexts. This may be done explicitly, particularly if it relates to curriculum knowledge. For example *high* means different things when used in different curriculum subjects: *high number, high musical note, high density, high position, high population*. An implication for teachers and speech and language therapists who work together is identifying key words in a subject area which may have a familiar meaning as well as a less familiar, technical, curricular meaning. In many situations the less familiar meaning may need to be explicitly explained. For example, in the maths or science lesson the familiar meaning of *table* can be identified and contrasted with the mathematical meaning and use of the word. Introducing new words which are synonyms can be helpful and may help avoid confusion since they employ the strategy mentioned earlier: one referent – one word label. Thus, rather than using *table*, synonyms such as *matrix* or *grid* could be introduced.

Words, particularly verbs, can become polysemous when they appear in different grammatical contexts. Phrasal verbs, such as *put* when it functions with a preposition, such as *put on, put away, put across*, have different meanings. A more subtle example is the polysemous meanings of *go*. *Go* may mean an action where the actor is going. It may also mean a state of being in place, as in *the book goes on the shelf.*

Most words are polysemous. The Cobuild Dictionary (1987) is based on meanings of words as they occur in regular use in speech and writing, rather than on decontextualised definitions of words. For example, in this dictionary the word *light* has thirty-six different meanings depending on the linguistic context, that is the words it is used with, e.g. *electric light, do you have a light? light a match, light blue, light-headed.* This dictionary is a great resource for teachers and speech and language therapists who are working in the area of meaning in language. Crystal (1987) outlines an approach which can be used by practitioners to teach vocabulary in support or intervention programmes.

Many words are polysemous because they have a literal meaning and a more abstract one. Children with semantic difficulties need support developing abstract meanings. For example, for the word *deep*, children may overextend the meaning of the word *big* to mean *deep*, before developing the meaning and the word *deep*. Children may need support and intervention to develop the more abstract meanings of *deep*, such as a descriptor of colour, breathing, gazing, thinking, debt, personality trait. There are implications for the way more abstract meanings of familiar and frequently used words are introduced to children and young people who have difficulties with word meanings.

We need more information about developmental patterns of naming and word learning. One study showed that 80 per cent of primary children with dyslexia are thought to show vocabulary difficulties (Wiig *et al.* 1982). Another study with 15-year-olds linked word learning and word understanding to reading proficiency (Nippold 1999). Pupils were asked to define abstract nouns, such as burden, gratitude, friendship, in writing. Pupils who were proficient readers performed better than their less proficient peers, by providing definitions that were accurate, precise and informative, reflecting the essential meaning of the word. There are implications for teaching word definition to pupils who are less proficient readers and who may have difficulties in learning abstract meanings of words. Speech and language therapists and teachers could work collaboratively on this approach.

Multi-word strings and formulaic sequences

Idiomatic forms of expression are particularly challenging for learners with semantic difficulties. Idioms are sayings, proverbs and multi-word strings, for example, *have a nice day, a watched pot never boils, it's like an oven in here*, as well as *take away* meaning *subtract*, or to be *skating on thin ice* meaning to be *in danger*. Idioms are chunks of language called **formulaic sequences** which are recognised and understood as a whole unit, an unanalysed 'chunk', with an idiomatic meaning. Nippold and Martin (1989 cited in Wray 2001) in their language development studies note that children younger than eight years old have a marked preference for analysing each word or morphological unit in a word string or series of utterances to help them derive grammatical and lexical information. However, older children and adults progressively organise language into less analysed chunks of multi-word strings, formulaic sequences. They propose that this change in strategies is because less analysis of multi-word strings and formulaic sequences results in quicker processing. Furthermore, other studies suggest that older children become more aware of the speech patterns of others and deal with language holistically rather than analytically (Wray and Perkins 2000 cited in Wray 2001).

Many individuals who have difficulties with the meaning of language may not understand or use multi-word strings as 'chunks' which are understood holistically. Consequently, they have difficulty understanding and using idiomatic meaning. One hypothesis is that they segment the idiom, saying or multi-word string and understand each word separately. When this process operates with idiomatic expressions, and multi-word strings, the underlying meaning of the 'chunk' is inaccessible, appearing to give a 'literal' meaning to the phrase (Wray 2001). Thus the teacher's chivvy to the dawdling pupil, '*pull up your socks*' produces a literal, over-analysed response from the child.

The processes of **collocating** and **coordinating** words also leads to 'chunking' which results in handling the meaning of language in a more holistic way and leads to faster processing. Both collocation and coordination concern word association based on the mutual expectancy of each word. Children, in retrieving words in response to word stimuli, tend to select words which often co-occur grammatically, that is collocation, so that they anticipate *dark/night,* and *table/eat* as 'chunks'. On the other hand, older learners retrieve words which are from the same word class as the stimuli, and are coordinates of the words presented, so that they anticipate *dark/light,* and *table/chair* as 'chunks' (Aitchison 1994).

As part of an assessment process, word elicitation tasks could show how children and young people with difficulties are storing and retrieving the meaning of idioms and other multi-word strings. Assessment could identify the ways in which the child was using analytical and holistic processing and this information would influence support and intervention.

This concludes the discussion of development and difficulties in aspects of meaning in language concerning vocabulary. We now discuss the grammatical aspects of meaning in language.

Word classes and parts of speech

When lexemes function within utterances and sentences they are governed by the rules of grammar. So a lexeme may operate within a clause as a subject, verb, object, adverb, and within a phrase as, say, an adjective, preposition, or adverb. In this way we can describe words not only by their meaning but also by their grammatical function, that is their **word class** or **part of speech**.

Traditionally, there are eight recognised word classes: nouns, pronouns, adjectives, verbs, adverbs, prepositions, conjunctions and interjections:

Nouns are the names of places, persons and things;
Pronouns are the words which may replace nouns or be used instead of them;
Adjectives modify nouns;
Verbs describe actions, states of being and events;
Adverbs modify verbs and also adjectives and other adverbs;
Prepositions indicate relationships between the nouns or pronouns which govern them and some other part of speech;
Conjunctions join clauses together;
Interjections express some kind of emotion.

Critical comment on this description of word classes argues that it is an insufficient framework for describing the grammatical function of words (Wardhaugh 1995; Aitchison 1994). Two main reasons which are generally cited are firstly, that these categories do not differentiate enough the grammatical functions of words, particularly the adverb category which has been described as a 'rag bag' category (Aitchison 1994) for words which do not belong in the other seven categories. Secondly, and more importantly, words will change their grammatical function, and thus their word class, depending on the function they have in the utterance. That is, words can be grammatically grouped either by how they look, their surface form, or according to how they perform in the utterance, so called distribution. For example, consider the grammatical function of the word 'singing' in these three utterances:

(i) The choir is singing in the Town Hall tonight.
(ii) The Singing Nun has made another record.

(iii) Singing does tremendous things for you.

In (i) 'singing' functions as a verb while in (ii) 'singing' functions as an adjective and in (iii) 'singing' functions as a noun.

Children in their language development seem to prefer to develop familiar, frequently occurring items in different word classes, assigning each word one grammatical function in their system. Gradually, most children learn that a word, as in the example above, may have several grammatical functions. For children with difficulties of meaning in language, assigning different grammatical roles to the same word depending on how it is operating in an utterance or sentence, may need specific support and intervention.

However, many children encounter difficulties understanding text where words may take on unfamiliar roles, such as when verbs become adjectives. Compare:

(i) The queen was crowned.
(ii) The crowned heads of Europe.

Yet this kind of text is very common in secondary school textbooks. Moreover, because of this difficulty, some children and adolescents may never use this form of words in their written language and it may need to be explicitly addressed in the classroom.

Open and closed classes of words

Another approach to looking at the grammaticality of words is along the lines of open and closed classes of words, that is words which are **content** words and those which are grammar or **function** words. Consider the utterance:

Some small children are playing in the park.

The content words are *small, children, play, park* and the function words are *some, are, in,* and *the*. Some children who have difficulties in retrieving words and structures may retrieve content words without function words and their utterances will be 'telegrammatic'. This retrieval difficulty may be because of the lack of content or lexical meaning in many of the function words. Their meaning derives from the grammatical structure they are supporting, which suggests that intervention based on meaning might be difficult in developing the use of function words. Alternatively, the explanation may be phonological. Function words may be more difficult to access and retrieve because they have a different, often weaker, phonological stress pattern than content words (Aitchison 1994), in which case intervention might take a phonological, word stress approach.

Grammatical themes of lexemes

It is widely thought that at the same time as learning the meaning of a word, the child also learns its grammatical role within an utterance. That is, we learn to assign meaning and grammatical role to words from the context of the utterance and interchange. For example, in an utterance some words are assigned the role of Subject or Object when they refer to people or things doing the action or being acted upon, while other words would be assigned the role of Adverb if they were situating the action in time, manner or place. Furthermore, there are particular grammatical meaning roles in an utterance which require other roles in order to make the meaning clear. For example, some verbs (doing, experiencing, being words) need a particular structure in which to operate; verbs such as *put, give, show* grammatically require a Subject, an Object and an Indirect Object or Adverb around them in order to make an acceptable grammatical utterance in English. In contrast, *walk* requires only a Subject and possibly an Adverb but no Object or Indirect Object. Difficulties in learning grammatical roles of words would result in unusual and unacceptable grammatical structures. As yet, this type of difficulty is rarely documented in the literature of child language research, although it is a feature of the language of children with semantic difficulties.

Meaning relations

A sentence or utterance not only has a grammatical structure but also a meaning structure. The meaning relation can be maintained even when the grammatical structure changes because the relationship between the lexical meaning is maintained. For example:

   (i) The person drove the car down the road.
   (ii) The car was driven down the road by the person.
   (iii) The car drove down the road.

The relationship between *the person, the car, driving* and *the road* are maintained. Some children with difficulties in this aspect of meaning cannot manipulate the grammatical structures and at the same time maintain the meaning relation. Furthermore, when the surface structure changes, they find it hard to understand that the meaning relation remains the same. This is shown particularly in the structures in (i) and (ii) above which are **passive** and **active** structures.

This concludes an overview of the way in which meaning in language develops in children and young people through learning content and grammatical meaning of words. In the last part of the chapter, we will focus more on difficulties in meaning in language. Two perspectives which are commonly referred to in discussions about difficulties in meaning in language are the **linguistic** and the **cognitive neuropsychological** perspectives. Linguistic and cognitive processing perspectives can help us to describe and understand the nature of difficulties in this area of language. Most researchers and practitioners draw on both perspectives to understand development and difficulties in meaning in language. We now look at these two perspectives.

Perspectives on meaning in language

A linguistic perspective

The linguistic approach describes the organisation of words as well as the roles of grammatical and meaning relations we assign them in contexts of utterances and interchange. Descriptions of language show how meaning in language operates at word level and at utterance level. The word is an important vehicle for expressing meaning, and words are organised in identifiable ways within the individual's language system. Meaning in language is also carried within a sentence or utterance through **grammatical roles**, such as Subject and Object, as well as **meaning relations**, which is the relation the action has with the actor and the thing acted upon. With linguistic descriptions of how words and utterances express meaning we can note difficulties which children have. Many pupils show some difficulties in understanding and expressing meaning in language while a smaller group show substantial and persistent difficulties which indicate a need for further detailed description and additional support and intervention.

A cognitive psycholinguistic perspective

A cognitive psycholingustic perspective allows us to investigate how meaning in language is processed. This approach explores the processing of meaning in language by looking at storage, access and retrieval strategies for words, grammatical relations and meaning. Looking at the development of words and meaning relations we may hypothesise that children employ strategies to store, access and retrieve meaning in language. Assessment can show whether a child's linguistic behaviours are typical of other children at a particular language level. We can also hypothesise that when these processes break down, assessment will identify where and how the breakdown happens and indicate possible avenues for intervention or support. Yet Dockrell *et al.* (1998: 453) caution that we need information about developmental patterns in naming and that, as yet, the underlying causes of semantic difficulties are unclear.

Types of difficulty with meaning

In this section we will look at a selection of difficulties which children may have with words and meaning: word-finding difficulties; using 'empty' lexis, and making-up words.

Word-finding difficulties

Children are considered to have word-finding difficulties when they have difficulty producing a target word in conversation, or when shown a picture, even though they have shown they recognise and understand the word (Dockrell *et al.* 1998). In a small survey done by Dockrell *et al.* (1998) they found that about 25 per cent of children with speech and language difficulties had word-naming difficulties involved. They noted that the causes of word-finding difficulties are not known but it is widely believed to be due to an inability to access and retrieve words. Children are usually slow to respond to the task, show difficulties in tasks which demand specific responses and tasks which are open-ended.

   The following language behaviours are usually shown in children with word-finding difficulties (Wiig *et al.* 1982; Landells 1989: 135).

- Stereotypic starters: 'and then' or 'and after that'.
- Pauses of over five seconds within one or more phrases in an utterance.
- Semantically empty place-holders:'uh', 'uhm'; or stereotyped phrases: 'well you know'.
- Using a 'filler' or empty word, e g. 'Serve *thingies* to cook'.
- Repeated repetitions of words and phrases in an utterance; self-correcting, starting, stopping and restarting e.g. 'A woman is going in . . . a woman is going . . . in the station'.

- Using several related words and phrases or giving a definition (circumlocution), e.g. 'I see one of them, Mrs Walker got'.
- Using initial speech sounds or silent articulatory gestures preceding the target word, such as mouthing the sound before saying it.
- Gesturing, signing, miming or using symbolic noise.
- Frustration gestures.

Landells suggests that the child's most effective search behaviours should be identified and the child encouraged to use them when there is a word-finding difficulty. When children do not have a word-searching strategy they may need to be taught one. For example, let the child know that their selected word was not appropriate and then prompt them to search for the correct one, such as using words related to the target word,

I've lost my . . . round . . . plastic . . . for drink . . . cup. I've lost my cup.

Dockrell *et al.* (1998) identify several intervention approaches used by practitioners:

- general vocabulary building as well as vocabulary building through semantic and phonological routes;
- memory training;
- phonological cues and semantic cues;
- non-verbal strategies;
- link word to a picture;
- increase child's confidence.

Empty lexis

Retrieval is facilitated by the familiarity and frequency of use of the lexeme. Children with difficulties may retrieve words which have a high frequency usage but low specificity of meaning, such as *got, have, put, do* and *thingie*. These items are known as 'empty' lexis. Reliance on 'general, all-purpose' verbs has been reported to characterise specific language difficulty (cited in Thordardottir and Weismer 2001). One suggested purpose of 'empty' lexemes is that they support the structure of the utterance and maintain the flow of conversation.

Information about use of non-specific vocabulary in typical development suggests that 'general, all-purpose' ('empty') verbs may be a feature of typical language development. In a recent study (Thordardottir and Weismer 2001), typically developing seven-year-old children show no differences in their use of 'general, all-purpose' verbs from peers with specific language difficulties. The authors claim that this supports the idea that using high frequency verbs helps establish meaning categories, and allows grammar and meaning structures to develop without loss of meaning. This is a similar hypothesis to the one used to explain the behaviour of children with language difficulties. However, 'empty' lexis may also mask a lack of content in the child's talking, placing an onus on the listener to enhance the content, either through shared knowledge, imagination or through more specific questioning. Having to ask searching questions often reveals the 'emptiness' of the child's lexis.

Making up words

When word-finding strategies are not successful children may invent their own words. For example, one child who was unable to retrieve the lexeme 'track suit top' called it a *zip jumper*, while another child called a 'tap' a *water handle*. Other children may use words which may be similar in meaning or in perceptual features; for example one girl called a 'paintbrush' a *pencil*. There are some children who access a word which is phonologically near the target word, for example, 'Mrs Watkins' is retrieved as *Mrs Hopkins*, and 'dairy' as *diary*. For other children the phonological form of the word, while following English phonological rules, will be a nonsense word; for example, one girl said *camerol* for the target word 'caramel'. Some children will make up completely nonsense words, such as *glom* and *drubble*.

Substantial and persistent difficulties of the kind that we have described in this chapter can lead quickly to communication breakdown and for this reason we identify this group of children as having difficulties with meaning and communication, or semantic-pragmatic difficulties. We discuss the nature of difficulties in communication in the next chapter.

Assessment

This section looks at assessing vocabulary and at specific assessment procedures concerning meaning in language.

Vocabulary assessment

Vocabulary is sensitive to the topic it concerns and to collect half an hour of a child's talk about animals would not do justice to the child's wider vocabulary range. In fact, samples of a child's talk always need to be collected from a variety of contexts, and this is particularly so for vocabulary. They may be collected from different people and situations in the classroom, across curriculum subjects, in different situations in the school and outside, as well as at home. For preschool children or older pupils with little expressive spoken language parents may be asked to keep a diary record of the words said by the child and the context in which they occurred, so that the meaning is as clear as possible. For pupils who have a large vocabulary, maybe only new or unusual words need to be recorded. As wide a range of vocabulary as possible should be collected to do justice to the individual's lexical development and any processing difficulties. The research studies of child vocabulary development show that we usually considerably underestimate the vocabulary range of children, both those with and those without difficulties in learning vocabulary (Wagner 1985 cited in Landells 1989; Crystal 1987).

Testing procedures

There are several commercially available assessment procedures for investigating development and difficulties with meaning in language. Since there is little information available on the development of aspects of meaning in language, many procedures are descriptive or task-based. Two linguistic descriptive procedures are called 'the Profile in Semantics – Grammar', and 'the Profile in Semantics – *Lexis*' (Crystal 1983). A third procedure is the *Test of Word Finding* (German 1986) which was developed in the United States and has items with American terms. This procedure focuses on what is known as *confrontation naming*, naming an item on demand, which, as discussed earlier, can be a stressful approach for individuals who have semantic difficulties.

Analysis of spontaneous vocabulary use and word-finding strategies may be preferable. Indeed, the relationship between tests for semantic language behaviours and children's semantic knowledge in conversational language in daily life is of central importance. A recent study (Ukrainetz and Blomquist 2002) with preschoolers showed that there was a statistical validity across four vocabulary tests and spontaneous language samples. However, there was considerable variation in the individual children's test scores, indicating that we need to be cautious about using these vocabulary tests to predict vocabulary and meaning in conversational language, particularly with children with semantic difficulties.

Support and intervention

Many teachers feel that linking work between cognitive development and lexical development is beneficial for the support of the child with semantic difficulties. This is in line with many programmes and materials available in primary school. For many children and older pupils who have shown some difficulties in the areas we have discussed, these programmes may be sufficient and successful. However, for a small group of children their difficulties lie less in their cognitive and intellectual development and more in specifically storing, accessing and retrieving meaning in language through linguistic organisation either at word level, utterance level or at both levels. Support and intervention with these pupils needs to focus on developing their linguistic strengths and strategies in order to manage their persistent difficulties.

Conclusion

We have looked at meaning in language in several ways. Linguistically, meaning in language can be described through words and their network of sense relations to each other as well as through grammatical functions and relations. Developmentally, children acquire words through salience and meaning, where their language meets the world around them. They acquire meaning relations in utterances by learning to manipulate grammatical structures in order to maintain the underlying meaning. When children learn words they learn both their meaning and their grammatical aspects.

Developmentally, it seems that children learn to process meaning in language by different strategies of storing, accessing and retrieving words which gradually become more efficient. Children and young people experience difficulties in the areas of processing as well as in organisation of their vocabulary and meaning. Assessment of these difficulties needs to go beyond word counts. Assessment needs to identify the aspects of meaning and processing giving rise to difficulty. Support can be effectively carried out by teachers and other practitioners through cognitive organisation tasks as well as through pupil-centred approaches, such as word-finding strategies.

Further reading

Aitchison, J. (1994) *Words in the Mind* (2nd edn). Oxford: Blackwell.

Chapter 7

Difficulties using language

Introduction

This chapter deals with difficulties in **pragmatics** which, in Bloom and Lahey's model, is the **Use** of language. Pragmatics concerns how we use the structures of language to make meanings in context; that is, using form to function appropriately. Utterances mean more than the meanings of the words we use. The social context in which utterances are made allows speakers and listeners to add inferences and implications which are drawn from knowledge of social interactions and knowledge of the world. Consequently, difficulties in using language are due as much to children's difficulties in understanding language meaning as to cognitive and emotional understanding of communicative appropriateness in social contexts.

In this chapter, we start by describing some of the linguistic and social characteristics of using language appropriately. We go on to discuss how children manifest difficulties in using language, and how practitioners can assess and support pragmatic difficulties in the classroom.

Linguistic characteristics of using language

Using language appropriately results in effective communication. It depends on both speakers and listeners using grammatical and semantic aspects of language which is informed by cognitive and conceptual knowledge of the world. In addition, they must bring to bear their emotional and social knowledge.

Grammatical features of language use

There are four main grammatical devices which we use to maintain effective communication, in conversation and narrative. They are **reference, substitution,**

ellipsis and **conjunctions**, and together they 'glue' the discourse together into a communicative whole (grammatical **cohesion**). Individual utterances are linked to each other to avoid repetition, maintain listener attention and to build on shared understanding so that the whole discourse makes communicative sense (Halliday and Hasan 1976).

Reference allows information to be carried across from previous utterances to subsequent ones, or to anticipate information, using grammatical short forms. For example, recurring words and phrases are referred to by pronouns, and *do/did* for a verb, *then* for time, *here/there* for place. This device avoids repetition and makes communication more effective. Consider this exchange:

Did your student read the book *Language Development in the Preschool Years?*
Yes my student did read the book *Language Development in the Preschool Years.*
What did your student think of the book *Language Development in the Preschool Years?*

Contrast with:

Did your student read the book *Language Development in the Preschool Years?*
Yes *she did.*
What did *she think* of *it?*

Substitution: We may substitute similar vocabulary to avoid repeating ourselves. For example:

He brings his little *puppy* into school and the teacher allows him to take his *pet* into the classroom.

Ellipsis is a device to avoid repetition when the conversation participants have a mutual understanding of information. For example:

Are you going to the park this afternoon?
Yes I am going to the park this afternoon.

Compare with:

Are you going to the park this afternoon?
Yes *I am.*

Conjunctions are grammatical words which join two or more utterances together, again to avoid repetition.

(i) The milk turned sour. The cream turned sour. The yoghurt turned sour.
(ii) The milk, cream and yoghurt turned sour.

These four grammatical devices help to make conversations and narratives as well as written language more communicatively effective. Pupils with difficulties using language may show difficulties with grammatical cohesion in spoken and written language and require a specific support programme.

Coherence

Conversation and narratives must not only make grammatical sense, they must also make sense socially and in linguistic meaning. There are three important aspects: speaker's intentions, shared understanding, and social appropriateness through inference and implication.

Speaker's intention: speakers must intend to speak for a particular purpose, such as asking a question, or intending to deny.

Shared understanding: speakers and listeners must have a shared understanding of the context for their utterances which depends on their understanding of the people to whom they are speaking and responding.

Inference and implication: speakers and listeners must understand and use appropriate politeness forms and conventions, such as in greetings, requests and questions. They must also understand and use the contextually determined meanings of words and phrases. For example, meanings can be inferred, as in: *It's stuffy in here* may be a polite request to open a window. Meanings can also be implied, as in: *The colour blue doesn't suit Jason*, which implies that Jason should not wear blue clothes.

Learners who have difficulties with these aspects of meaning in conversation, narratives and written texts, will usually show their difficulties by responding inappropriately and being unable to maintain a meaningful exchange.

Conversational skills

Conversation is the most frequent and familiar form of speech and language activity, and we can identify a variety of characteristics which are necessary for a conversation to take place:

Topic: the speaker should be able to introduce, maintain and conclude a topic of conversation.

Turn-taking: exchanging turns in speaking and listening as well as changing the topic in a conversation is a fundamental skill.

Manner of address: the manner of speaking to your conversational partner, whether it is formal or informal, as well as the volume and tone is important.

Repair: when the conversation breaks down because of misunderstanding, hesitancy or interruption, then the listener should be able to seek clarification and the speaker should be able to repair the break.

Effective communication: the utterance, message or conversation should convey what the speaker intends it to.

Appropriate grammatical structures: the speaker should be able to use the appropriate grammatical forms to express the information, such as those described above for cohesion and coherence.

Non-verbal communication: facial expressions, gestures, body language and body space need to be appropriately matched to the spoken language.

We need to consider these areas in more detail, exploring the nature of the difficulties shown in each area and some approaches to supporting and intervening with the pupil. While we deal with them separately here, these characteristics are interrelated.

Topic

Children or young people with difficulty in topic skills are noticeable in two ways: either they present a degree of restlessness caused by constantly changing topic and not maintaining any one topic for long. Alternatively, they may appear terse because of their succinct responses to any topic overtures without extending the topic which has been introduced, or introducing any new topic.

A primary skill which needs to be established is the ability to understand when a topic is introduced, which is often signalled by open-ended questions. Pupils with difficulties managing topic can be encouraged to recognise these signals. Once recognition of topic is possible then strategies for maintaining the topic can be practised, such as through further questions and comments from their own experience.

An initial strategy might be to agree with the pupil about how many exchanges (questions/replies) would be acceptable which would set a framework within which performance could be monitored. Encourage the pupils to initiate topics from areas they are interested in and, when they digress in group conversation, bring them back to the topic but note what topics they digress on to and return to them for fuller conversation at another time. Some children may have difficulty ending the topic of conversation and they need to be made aware of when and how others do this and enabled to adopt similar strategies. For example, saying, *That's great. Now I'd like to change the subject*, or *I have to go now*, gives feedback about their performance which is appropriate and consistent.

It is also important to remember that initiating and maintaining conversation may vary across different cultural groups. For example, in some Asian communities it may be considered impolite for a child to initiate a topic of conversation with an adult.

Turn-taking

Taking turns in communication is a feature of human interaction from the cradle. Games like Peekaboo encourage infants to take turns in listening, waiting for their communication turn and then taking it when it is offered. Most children readily learn the skill. Those who have difficulties in turn-taking usually show it by not taking their turn in conversations, by pre-empting their turn and interrupting, or by not relinquishing their turn and monopolising the conversation. They often find telephone conversations extremely difficult to maintain. Turn-taking can be taught, often by making the individual aware of appropriate grammatical signals, such as questions, pause and intonation. Pupils with difficulty sharing the changing of topic often change topic unexpectedly which usually precipitates conversation breakdown. They need to be made aware of the signals which indicate that a change of topic is imminent and to listen for them and use them themselves. For example, *by the way, to change the subject*, or an extended pause.

Manner of address

Sometimes this group of children and young people have difficulties using the appropriate style, or register, of language, that is, they may be friendly to strangers, condescending to adults, or they may adopt a formal or authoritarian style with their peers. These individuals have not learnt to do what most other children learn, and that is to place the people they interact with into appropriate categories, or registers, for language style. If they do this, they can address both familiar and new people appropriately. Individuals who use an inappropriate manner of address need immediate feedback, pointing out the inappropriateness of the style and offering an alternative model. This needs to be done within a consistent framework otherwise this group of pupils may begin to feel unsuccessful as communicators.

Repair

When the conversation breaks down because of misunderstanding, hesitancy or interruption, then the listener should be able to seek clarification and the speaker should be able to repair the break. Individuals who experience conversational difficulties are rarely able to do this, and they rely on the more able conversational partner to recognise breakdown and to repair it. Their parents, teachers and therapists are usually well practised at repairing and maintaining these conversations which gives a false sense of conversational competence to the individual with difficulties. When breakdown occurs it is a good strategy to make these individuals aware of it and to seek clarification about the repair, by saying, for example, *I don't understand;* **who** *gave you the book?*

Effective communication

Communicating effectively means that the speaker is conveying what he or she intends to say and what the conversational partner would be expected to understand, given the situational context. When the meaning to be conveyed is mutually shared, such as an activity or picture in the here-and-now, then communication is more likely to be successful. However, when the meaning is more abstracted, concerning an event at another time in another place, which only the speaker was involved in, or concerns imagining what might happen next in a story or a hypothetical situation, then the challenge to communicate effectively is much more difficult.

In many cases, individuals with difficulties in using language cannot manipulate language sufficiently to convey abstract information, particularly concerning inferring meaning about possible events or about people's feelings and emotions, and also linking cause and effect. Often their ability to verbally reason is logical but idiosyncratic and confusing to their conversational partner. Consequently, accessing certain aspects of curriculum subjects, such as History, English literature or Science, is difficult. While there are activities and programmes which support and develop this aspect of expressive difficulty, it may be necessary to establish awareness and understanding of these concepts. Because their understanding about inferences and empathy is sometimes in doubt, many of these children may be considered to have emotional and personality difficulties along the pragmatic-autism continuum.

Appropriate grammatical structures

While many children with difficulties in the area of pragmatics have no problems with grammar, they may not use the grammatical structures to communicate effectively. For example, they may not be able to convey to their conversational partner what information is new and what is familiar and 'old'. They may start to talk about new information without naming the new items and only use pronouns. This feature of their expressive language can seriously jeopardise communication, such as recalling an event or a feedback activity to the teacher or class group. Clarification by the listener has to be sought if communication is to be repaired and maintained.

Non-verbal communication

Non-verbal communication includes facial expressions, gestures, body language and body space and they should be appropriately matched to the spoken language. If they are not then two messages are being sent by the speaker, which is confusing. It is important to remember that non-verbal communication is largely culturally determined and varies across different communities and societies. This has implications for assessment and the nature of any support or intervention.

Types of difficulty using language

There is debate about identifying and distinguishing difficulties in using language, that is social language (pragmatic) difficulties, and semantic-pragmatic language difficulties or disorders (SPLD). There is some agreement that there are similarities between children with SPLD and children on the autistic spectrum (e.g. Boucher 1998). Recent studies have sought to distinguish between the language difficulties of children with SPLD and children who only have pragmatic difficulties. However, children with difficulties in these areas often present with similar language behaviours. In conversation they may have poor turn-taking skills and difficulty staying on topic and they may not always take into account the knowledge of their conversational partner. They may have subtle comprehension difficulties, tending to be over-literal and their ability to infer can be restricted or delayed in development (Smedley cited in Adams 2001: 290).

Bishop (2000) has tried to identify some distinguishing features. She argues that children with pragmatic language difficulties do not necessarily have autistic behaviours. Importantly, there is high variation among children with pragmatic difficulties and practitioners need to look for signs of overlap with autism rather than expect them. Children with pragmatic difficulties have primary difficulties in communication and conversation but may not have additional language difficulties in other aspects of language, such as grammar.

Children with SPLD have primary difficulties with semantic knowledge as well as possible difficulties with grammar (Bishop and Adams 1989). They have difficulties with learning vocabulary, word-finding and auditory comprehension (see Chapter 6). They are often described either as relatively quiet and under-confident, or as relatively verbose because of conversational strategies to hide their struggle to retrieve words (Adams 2001: 291).

Children with difficulties in semantics and social language use have long-term needs academically and socially. Poor communication skills restrict socialising with peers and lead to decreasing social participation often resulting in exclusion from social groups in later life. Facilitating communicative interaction skills and support for families in the early and school-age years is an important part of intervention (Adams 2001: 291).

Background information

In many instances, pupils with difficulties in the social use of language have a similar pattern of language development. It is not unusual that they are identified as having persistent difficulties in using language when they are in their middle childhood, in junior school. Their developmental history shows that they usually start to talk comparatively late, often after three years of age. Yet, once they begin to talk, they usually develop clear, fluent speech and sentences. They show difficulties in understanding language which remains a persistent feature of their communication. Usually when the demands of curriculum learning become more dependent on language and literacy, these pupils' difficulties show through. Their difficulties in understanding language are usually at a comparatively high level of language functioning and their expressive language shows inappropriateness and lacks cohesion. Often further assessment is requested because the adults involved with the child suspect that he or she may have learning, emotional or language difficulties. Depending on the severity of the difficulties in using language, some children may show emotional and learning difficulties as well, throughout their early development.

Assessment

Children with difficulties in social use of language usually perform as well as their peers on formal tests of grammar, phonology, naming and word reading but less well on understanding language and narrative tasks. It is important to distinguish between children with pragmatic difficulties, and children whose primary difficulties are in understanding language which give rise to difficulties communicating. One assessment, the *Children's Communication Checklist* (Bishop 1998) aims to identify this distinction by rating communication and social behaviour and identifying social difficulties, in addition to language problems.

To distinguish between children's difficulties in social language use and difficulties with semantic aspects of language, practitioners need to assess children's general vocabulary development, through procedures such as the *British Picture Vocabulary Scales* (BPVS) (Dunn *et al.* 1982) and the *Test for Word Finding* (German 1986). They may also wish to explore general learning abilities, e.g. through the *British Abilities Scale* (Elliott 1996).

An investigation of communicative behaviour for very young children with communication difficulties can be carried out through the child's parents or main caregivers. One procedure is given in *The Pragmatics Profile of Everyday Communication Skills in Children* (Dewart and Summers 1995). It gathers valuable information about how, when, to whom and what the child communicates in the home. It may also be carried out interviewing nursery or school staff for information about communicative behaviour there. It can be carried out in English, Panjabi and Bengali.

Assessment of understanding of language use in the junior school or older pupil needs to go beyond comprehension of simple grammatical structures. This group of pupils will not usually show difficulties at that level. Their difficulties lie in understanding complex sentences which require processing and this can be assessed through the *Test for the Reception of Grammar* (TROG) (Bishop 1983).

There are two further assessments for older primary and secondary mainstream pupils with pragmatic difficulties: *The Social Use of Language Programme* (SULP) has a Communication Skills Rating Chart (Rinaldi 1992) and the *Clinical Evaluation of Language Fundamentals Test* (CELF –R UK) (Semel *et al.* 1997).

There are three important informal approaches to assessing social language use in children and identifying difficulties: narrative, conversation and referential communication.

Narrative: Children with higher-level language difficulties show an inability to structure a sequence of ideas into connected discourse, although they may show no grammatical errors (Adams 2001). Stories retold by this group of children differ from those of their peers by being shorter, with fewer cohesive ties, fewer linguistic features indicating time and cause-effect relationships, and including less, or wrong, information (Merritt and Liles 1989 and Weaver and Dickinson 1982 cited in Adams 2000). Consequently, retelling stories as an assessment procedure may be a particularly sensitive measure which identifies key language difficulties for children with pragmatic difficulties. It can also be used to measure progress over time in the school years.

Conversation: Looking at conversation skills of children with pragmatic difficulties can provide a descriptive communicative profile of language behaviours such as turn-taking, responsiveness and initiation of topics. This profile can serve as a baseline to plan and evaluate support and intervention.

Referential communication: Children with pragmatic difficulties can find it hard to communicate information efficiently. A procedure to assess this skill takes the form of a barrier game in which partners are asked to give each other instructions to perform a task. In comparison with their peers, children with pragmatic difficulties make fewer requests for clarification of information (Leinonen and Letts 1997).

In addition, it can be helpful to use observation notes and audio/videotape-recorded information of the expressive language of children with pragmatic difficulties. Video-recorded information is important in language assessment of this group of pupils because of the need to investigate the non-verbal communication as well as the verbal. There is also the issue of language-situation mismatch. Information from observations and video recordings of pupils' play, social interactions and learning are valuable as indicators of the appropriateness of the meaning of language they are using. Where there is a mismatch between the situation and what the child is saying, communication is jeopardised.

Bearing in mind the social context of communicative behaviour, pupils with difficulties in the social use of language benefit from collaborative work between parents, teachers, speech and language therapists and educational psychologists in assessment procedures as well as support and intervention (see also Chapter 9).

Support and intervention strategies

Goals and plans for support and intervention depend on the profile of communicative language behaviours obtained from formal and informal assessment procedures. Support and intervention will be different according to whether the problem seems to be a semantic-pragmatic difficulty or a pragmatic difficulty. Adams (2001) describes interventions for two case studies illustrating both types of difficulties.

Child A was a ten-year-old boy with a history of severe receptive language delay and some behavioural and attention difficulties. Until he was five years old he showed little communicative intent, poor eye contact and insistence on sameness. He did not have hearing difficulties or traits of autism. Most of these difficulties have resolved and he is fluent but not verbose. A range of formal and informal assessments were carried and an analysis of A's conversation skills showed that he had difficulties maintaining relevant conversation and repairing breakdowns in conversation. Following discussion between the teacher, and speech and language therapist and others, specific intervention goals were identified:

- giving adequate information to the interlocutor;
- being concise;
- sequencing of events in narrative;
- use of prosody to convey meaning;
- interpretation of complex auxiliary and modal verbs.

The approach was developmental and a metapragmatic approach (Anderson-Wood and Smith 1997) which is 'helping the client to become consciously aware of communication rules and knowledge' (p.72); for example, seeking clarification when a response is not understood. This is often taught through role play and endorsed in conversation. After ten weeks of intervention, a second conversation analysis showed that there was an overall reduction in A's conversational difficulties.

Child B was seven years old and attending a child psychiatric unit when he was referred to speech and language therapy with alleged semantic-pragmatic language difficulties. Although he had had ear infections his hearing was now normal. He said his first words when he was four years old, and by five he was speaking in sentences and was discharged from speech and language therapy. He still uses gestures to support his speech, and he is frustrated by his inability to speak. His interaction with peers is poor and his interests narrowly focused, but he is not thought to have autistic traits.

On formal assessments, B's main difficulties showed in hesitating and false starts when speaking, errors in naming tasks in meaning and phonologically (phonological paraphasias). Phonetic cueing helped his performance. Naming items within a category was limited for his age. Non-word repetition was poor. He was able to group items by semantic category, suggesting he had difficulties in word retrieval rather than storing words. He participated in conversation although he became confused when the input level was complex. Retelling a story revealed a lower number of main ideas and information as well as difficulties in cohesion devices. These assessments showed that B's difficulties were linked more to semantic knowledge, understanding and word-finding difficulties which gave rise to pragmatic difficulties. Intervention goals focused on semantic and word-finding difficulties by strengthening phonological memory and word retrieval:

- strengthen phonological awareness skills;
- strengthen memory skills, in particular phonological memory skills;
- over-rehearse memory tasks and phonological awareness tasks;
- retrieve lists of alliterative words and rhymes;
- sequence ideas in narrative and conversation.

Adams does not note how long weekly intervention continued, but B's word-finding skills improved so that he performed similarly to his peers, and his narrative and conversational skills also improved. He became more confident in his conversations with others.

These two case studies illustrate the range of difficulties and intervention approaches which are needed for children with difficulties in semantic and pragmatic aspects of language. We need to turn now to examine the situational contexts which influence how we communicate. Although we are primarily concerned with the influences on children and young people with difficulties in the social use of language, much of what follows about communication in the home and classroom is relevant to all learners.

Social factors and development of communicative skills

The development of a substantial portion of communication skills is largely dependent on the communication behaviour of the community in which the child develops, be this in social class groups, in home and school and in language environments other than English. With regard to social class groups, Wells (1986) has shown that there is no evidence to support the long-held assumption that there is 'verbal deprivation' in families of lower socio-economic status. However, Wells, and Tizard and Hughes (1984) before him did go on to show that the home and the school expect substantially different sets of communication skills.

Bilingual children

Children who grow up in linguistic minority communities speaking their community language develop the communicative behaviour skills of their first language group. Some children acquire one language after the other and are described as sequential bilinguals. They usually bring the first language skills to the communicative behaviour of the second language where they may be seen as inappropriate. For example, initiating conversation or asking questions by a child to an adult may be acceptable in some language communities and unacceptable in others. A silent or minimally responsive child may be very acceptable in one language community while arousing suspicions and anxiety in another. Children who acquire both languages at the same time and so become bilingual simultaneously, seem to encounter fewer difficulties in acquiring the appropriate communicative behaviours for each language (Fantini 1985).

Further, many linguistic minority children face an additional challenge when acquiring the skills of communicative behaviour in a second language because they are acquiring these skills in a school environment which is different from the home.

School and class communicative behaviour

Teaching is not only a special form of conversing with others – it is an especially difficult form, if for no other reason than that the teacher must 'converse' with a large heterogeneous group of listeners (Wardhaugh 1985: 71). Analysis of the social context in which teachers and children communicate in the classroom looks at style, intent, purpose, and the context of communication.

Communication style

Studies (e.g. Wood 1988) have shown that the recurring communicative style in the classroom is one where the teacher is the powerful initiator and the pupils are the less powerful respondents. Wood (1988) refers to 'the nature of conversation and the important differences that exist between . . . relaxed talk with a friend and more stressful interactions with teachers' (p.138). He goes on to discuss the way in which 'questions asked in school "violate" many of the normal conventions' (p.139) surrounding the asking of questions and the questioned person's right to negotiate their manner of response. Teachers often know the answer to the questions they ask and will rarely tolerate more than a limited range of acceptable responses. He points out that not complying with this style of interaction can bring about a sense of failure which is both 'serious and threatening', and which increases as the pupil grows older.

Teachers may feel constrained by goals which must be achieved during their class time with the children, such as an attainment target in the subject area of the curriculum. Studies (Nuthall and Church 1973) have shown that the question-answer format of interaction can produce in pupils high levels of retention of factual information. Yet teachers are aware that this 'register' of interaction is limited both in terms of communicative development and effectiveness and also in terms of appreciation and understanding of the subject matter.

The question-answer-acknowledgement exchange has been observed as the main style of discourse in classrooms around the world both in nursery and in secondary age groups. Two studies, cited in Wood *et al.* (1986) show that the frequency of teacher questions as a proportion of all their utterances was similar (just under 50 per cent) in a UK nursery class and in an American high school class for 17-year-olds, while the incidence of pupils' questions was less than 8 per cent in both groups. Later in the book (Chapter 10) we look at this issue through a teaching activity.

There are two important features of this interactive format which have implications for children with language processing difficulties and learning difficulties. Firstly, there is the shortness of the response time allowed by teachers for pupils to answer the question. Research has shown that most teachers leave on average about one second for pupils to respond. When the 'wait time' is increased to about three seconds the quality of the pupils' responses improved, being 'more frequent, relevant, thoughtful and "high level"' (Rowe 1984 and Swift and Gooding 1983 cited in Wood *et al.* 1986). For pupils with difficulties understanding language then, a longer response time allowance is important. These pupils need more time to process oral language and to encode their own response to it.

Secondly, pupils with difficulties in communicative interaction may find their difficulties exacerbated in a question-answer format. All pupils and particularly those with difficulties using language need the opportunity to develop their own discourse skills and one way would be through peer interaction. Consequently, teachers are encouraged to 'move away from whole-class teaching and teacher domination of discourse', towards allowing pupils to develop their talk processes and 'metadiscoursal skills' (Hardman and Beverton 1993: 146).

Hardman and Beverton (1993) looked at the development of discourse skills in a group of Year 9 (13–14-year-old) mixed-ability pupils in a UK comprehensive school. Throughout the academic year the pupils were encouraged to discuss their project work in class, giving them the chance to raise their awareness about discourse. By the end of the year, discourse skills such as attentive listening, turn-taking, negotiation, topic maintenance, as well as sensitivity and empathy towards the listener/speaker, and cognitive skills shown by the pupils were similar to those achieved by older pupils recorded in other studies (Robinson 1990).

Questions can be most helpful when at the appropriate 'level of demand' for the pupils' abilities. A question such as 'What is this?' is at a low level of demand, while a question such as 'In the story, what might happen next?' is at a higher level of demand. The appropriateness of the level of demand for pupils with pragmatic difficulties is crucial to their progress.

Communicative purpose and intent

Most teachers find communication in class with their pupils constrained by the requirements of the curriculum. They may also feel constrained by their own notions and expectations of 'educating pupils'; that is, they may feel that the main task is information giving and eliciting between themselves and the pupils. This may be keenly felt in subject areas at secondary level. Further, teachers may feel constrained by time, or the lack of it, particularly in secondary schools where most teachers will only teach a group of pupils for less than two hours a week. The communicative purpose in any teaching session may well be focused on information giving by the teacher. All these factors inhibit rather than facilitate the teacher's identification of pupils in the class with communication difficulties. This identification would suggest more appropriate teaching approaches with communicative purposes wider than just information giving or eliciting. Wells (1986) gives two contrasting examples of two teachers' interaction with a young infant school child, showing clearly that a communicated interest in what the child has to say is a more effective motivator than an interest in the *accuracy* of information elicited.

Communicative context

Creating a supportive environment and appropriate context is essential for successful communication.

Home and school: Questions, demands and interaction will occur in both contexts but home seems to be a less stressful communicating environment according to comparative studies of school-age children talking at home and at school (Wells 1986). At home the children display a wider range of communicative competence and skill than they do at school. This in part may be due to the adult-child ratio being much smaller at home. Yet Wells' research shows that on many occasions the teachers ignored the children's communication and efforts to contribute to discussion.

Abstract and activity contexts: It has been noted (Child 1982) that children will communicate more successfully when the context centres around some activity, particularly when it is building up and knocking down – 'build 'n bash', but also around pictures, books and stories. Moreover, this is associated with ethnicity and social class. As pointed out earlier, an abstract context, away from the 'here and now', makes more demands on children's communicative abilities, that is, they are required to describe the non-shared context with the teacher or their conversational partner both in time and space and to develop the sequence of events accurately or in an organised way to be understandable. They are also required to clarify any breakdown in understanding by repairing areas of breakdown in the abstract context. Pupils with difficulties using language find this extremely difficult. The interested reader is directed to McTear (1985) who gives some examples of this behaviour.

Communication partners: There are also differences noted in the communicative effectiveness due to communication partners. Children and young people will communicate better with some groups of people than with others. For example, they may talk more with their peer group than with their teachers, and within their peer group with certain friends. They may show the greatest difficulty communicating with identifiable authority figures or less familiar adults, such as the head teacher, the doctor, the dentist, the therapist, the educational psychologist, and show more communication skills with the dinner ladies and classroom assistants.

Situational context: Recognising that context plays an essential role in the communicative effectiveness of a pupil has implications for the assessment of communication skills in the pupil. The importance of context in the assessment of pragmatic and communicative language skills of pupils with difficulties using language is clearly described by Stacey (1994). She shows how the child performs very differently in the school, home and clinic contexts which has implications for understanding the nature of the difficulty and educational provision. Practitioners need to establish a pupil's communicative repertoire across the range of contexts in which the pupil operates. This is particularly important in the assessment of pragmatic skills of bilingual children. The repertoire of their skills will range across different languages as well as across the different contexts and interlocutors in the linguistic communities.

Conclusion

We have discussed in this chapter how we can make language do what we want it to. Children and young people who have difficulties in controlling language may also have difficulties in other areas of communication. Assessment is best done through observations from a range of sources in the pupils' communication contexts and collaboration between parents and practitioners is essential. Support and intervention for pupils with difficulty using language needs to be consistent, encouraging the pupils to reflect on what is being said to them and about the appropriateness of their response. Since many in this group of pupils may also have difficulties processing complex and abstract (inferential) language, they find aspects of the curriculum difficult to access. We have reviewed many ways in which practitioners need to be aware of the quality of their communication with these pupils. For example, the type of questions they ask, and how much time they allow for response, influence the quality and quantity of pupil communication in the classroom and can either exacerbate or ameliorate a pupil's difficulty.

Further reading

Andersen-Wood, L. and Smith, B.R. (1997) *Working with Pragmatics.* Bicester: Winslow.

Chapter 8

Comprehension difficulties

Introduction

In Chapter 2, we noted that in order to understand why some children have difficulties in learning language, practitioners are increasingly interested in examining the way in which language is processed. It was suggested that the processing of language can be viewed from the way a person takes in, or *decodes* language, and from the way that they produce or *encode* it – 'input' and 'output'. To some extent, these are represented by 'speaking and listening' which have become familiar for the examination of children's communication in school. Listening is one form of processing in which spoken language is 'taken in'. Speaking is the active processing of language 'output'.

Of course, we use other means too. Vision is important for taking in information and, to a lesser extent, touch is important. For some children who cannot rely on hearing and listening, vision and touch may be especially important. For most children, speaking and listening are inextricably linked and can be considered together. However, when children seem to be experiencing difficulty in communicating through language, it will be important to examine aspects of input and output separately to see if there are any clues to where the difficulties may lie. The taking in of information is the first stage in understanding. Adequate understanding or comprehension is essential for effective communication. In this chapter, we will consider some aspects of comprehension.

First, consider how we take in information from people and activities around us. We look, we listen and we feel, with our eyes and ears and with our hands and other parts of our bodies. We use our senses. In order to take in spoken language we mainly use our sense of hearing and our sense of vision. The use of our senses to take in information is known as perception and it relies heavily on learning and experience. We remember things we have seen before and we recognise sounds, for example tunes and people's voices, when we have heard them before. This ability to recognise and make sense of things seen and things heard develops as we get older and is essential to our understanding of the world.

How does understanding begin? There is a great deal of evidence that babies are already beginning to take in information at a very early age. Experiments with infants of just a few months old indicate that they show preference for human voices, in particular those of the mother or other familiar carers, and also prefer to look at faces rather than inanimate objects (Bower 1977). They appear to be 'pre-programmed' to take notice of other human beings. Furthermore, children's efficiency in searching for relevant information increases with age and further learning. This is clearly important as it is from other people that they will learn to talk and to behave in acceptable ways.

The development of attention

The first step towards understanding is attention. We need to pay attention to something before we can take in information from it and understand it. For most people, attention is selective. They select something to look at from a whole range of things to see; they listen to the person who is talking to them when there may be plenty of other noise around them. People select what is salient, or interesting to them and they pay attention to it. There are plenty of examples of this in daily life: a restaurant will stand out in a row of shops when we are hungry and looking for somewhere to eat; people can become so absorbed in their attention to a book that they fail to hear someone talking to them. Conversely, we 'switch off' our attention to a boring television programme or indeed, a boring speaker. We can also learn to hear things that we were previously unaware of, for example when studying music or learning a foreign language. In these examples, we are paying attention to something that is relevant and meaningful at that moment.

These examples suggest that to a great extent, attention is qualitative rather than quantitative. The length of time we attend to something relates very much to its interest level. It assumes a great deal to simply say that a person 'has a long attention span' because their attention will vary according to what there is to see or to hear. The comment needs to be qualified by explaining what it is that holds a person's attention for so long. The same applies to children. It is not helpful to say that a child has 'good concentration' or a 'long attention span' without saying what the child attends to or concentrates on. We need to know the quality of the attention and what controls it.

As with many aspects of human behaviour and learning, information about the context in which it occurs is crucial. Awareness of the development of attention control in young children is important in the study of language. Some children have difficulty in establishing and maintaining their attention in certain situations or the control of their attention may be as we would expect of a much younger child. This may be related to difficulties in learning to understand language. The development of attention will relate to a number of developing skills as a child matures and learns through experience. As we have said, attention to visual and auditory information will partly depend on the child's ability to see and to hear, that is, their auditory and visual acuity. However, they need to learn to use these senses and this may relate to other aspects of development. Auditory and visual perception to some extent relates to physical development. As a young baby acquires motor control, the ability to lift the head, turn around and move towards interesting objects will affect looking and listening. Understanding will develop as a child begins to associate things seen with things heard. The sound of food being prepared will often stimulate particular responses in a young child who may look towards the kitchen or move towards the site of the preparation.

Consider too the situation of answering the telephone. For most people, this activity requires a sound to be heard which is associated with an object, the telephone. The person then makes a movement towards the object in order to respond. Each of these activities begins with a focus of attention onto a particular sound and the final outcome depends on the overall comprehension of what is happening.

In the field of language development and language difficulty, some extremely useful guidelines on the development of attention were developed by Joan Reynell and her colleagues (Cooper *et al.* 1978). They identified stages of development of attention control and related this to children's language development and their learning in school.

Stage 1: This is the type of attention observable in young babies. They are extremely distractible and pay only momentary attention to the main stimulus of the moment. For example, the introduction of a musical toy, a moving object or an external noise such as an aeroplane will catch the baby's attention for a few seconds. In the very early stages, an infant's attention will be affected by the lack of control of their head and other movements as they will not be able to look at an object for long or turn towards a noise. At Stage 1 therefore, the control of attention is external to the child and at the mercy of their reflexes and the environment. It is easy to link this stage with the sensory-motor stage described by Piaget in which an infant's attention is action-dependent. There is no separation of a child's thinking from external activities (see Donaldson 1978).

Stage 2: At this stage, which develops in the second year of life, attention comes under the control of the child. However, the attention is rather fixed and inflexible as the child concentrates on something of interest and cannot easily be distracted to something else. It is difficult for an adult to 'break in'.

Stage 3: Now attention is beginning to move from the rigidity of Stage 2 and the child's attention can be drawn, by an adult, from one thing to another. However, Reynell and her colleagues described this level of attention as 'single-channelled' because there can be attention only to one thing at a time. There can be no division of attention and the child's whole visual and auditory interest must be gained. The control of the attention at this stage is with the adult.

Stage 4: The attention at this stage is under the child's own control although it can still be considered 'single-channelled'. The child is able to switch from one thing of interest to another but at any one time is concentrating on one thing only. At this stage it would be possible for an adult to attract a child's attention from a task in order to offer them some help. The child, however, would have to pay complete attention to the intervention before returning to the original focus of attention.

Stage 5: At this stage, a child is beginning to be able to take in some directions while engaged in a task, provided that the task and the direction are well within the child's understanding. If the instruction is too difficult, then the child reverts to single-channelled attention on one task.

Stage 6: At this stage, a child is able to integrate two 'channels' of attention. So for example, the child may be looking at something and listening to instructions for carrying out an activity at the same time. Reynell and her colleagues suggest that this is the type of attention control required for a child to learn in a class at school.

These descriptions of the development of attention can be helpful in making observations of children and they can suggest ways to assist children who may have difficulties in listening and understanding. For example, children at Stage 1 will be highly distractible and only pay attention to clear and simple sounds and objects. It will be necessary to use what is immediately interesting to the child and to reduce all other distractions to a minimum. At Stage 2, it will be almost impossible to distract a child from their immediate focus of attention. Such children may respond with distress if asked to change their activity or conform to the rest of the group.

At Stage 3, a child's attention will have to be focused before speaking to them or showing them something. It may be appropriate to turn the child's face towards a stimulus or to make them look directly at the person who is speaking.

Children at Stage 4 will often attend if asked to 'look' or 'listen' before showing or telling them something. They need to be alerted to something that is going to happen. In Stages 5 and 6, a child will usually pay attention provided they are interested in what is happening and that instructions are given at an appropriate level.

It is easy to see how attention affects understanding. A child who is distracted by every new sound or movement will have difficulty listening to instructions, as will a child whose attention is so rigid that it cannot be turned easily to something new. However, if we understand that a child needs to be alerted before an instruction is given, then there is every chance that they will look or listen and control their attention, provided they are interested in what is happening. Only if they are paying attention will they be able to take in information and understand it. In school learning, teachers usually determine and control what the focus of attention is to be. Through various strategies of classroom organisation and management, they attempt to maintain children's attention on tasks and, hopefully, guide them to completion.   Many teachers are aware of pupils who never seem to listen and who always seem to be fidgeting when required to sit still. It may be useful to try to place them at one of the levels described above and to gradually attempt to develop their attention skills through the stages. The explanation for why they never seem to follow instructions or conform to the rest of the group could be that the level of their attention is at an earlier stage of development than other pupils'.

We said earlier that learning and experience are important in the development of perception and that attention is the first step to taking in information and understanding it. This may lead us to think why some children have difficulty in controlling their attention. It is possible that for some children, opportunities to learn may not have been available. The most obvious examples will be found in children who do not see or hear very well. They may have difficulty in focusing on the most important, or salient object or sound. The child who does not hear well may not learn to associate sound with meaning. Some children may be delayed in this aspect of learning if they have experienced temporary or intermittent loss of hearing, perhaps through frequent ear infections in their early years. It is also thought that in some children, the maturation of the nervous system takes longer and that they show slower development in learning to listen, pay attention and therefore understand.

Observing attention

The assessment of a child's attention control will be an important element of the assessment of their understanding and, indeed, it will be important to ascertain, as far as possible, whether the problem is one of attention or of understanding. There will be some children who do pay attention but who still cannot comprehend what is said. As with other aspects of language assessment, it is only by observing the child in a number of situations that we can gain an idea of their ability to pay attention and take in information.

It will also be necessary to note the behaviour of other people, including those who care for a child at home. How do they gain the child's attention? How much background noise is there, or other potentially distracting visual stimuli? In order to gain a picture of a child's attention skills, try to observe them over time, in different circumstances. Note precisely what attracts their attention, that is, which objects, people, sounds and activities they seem to be most interested in. If possible, say how long the child pays attention to each stimulus. Over a period of several observations it should be possible to categorise the things that attract the child's attention and those which hold it.

- Are they for example, all brightly coloured objects?
- Are they mainly non-language-related sounds, such as aeroplanes overhead or other noises outside the room?
- Does the child pay attention to an individual person and not when with several people in a group?
- Is it children or adults that attract the child's attention? Which children? Which adults?

Further analysis of the observations might suggest that the child mainly pays attention to visual rather than auditory stimuli. This information may be helpful in planning for the child's learning. They may respond to visual clues and these may help them in the transition to listening to sounds and voices.

In identifying a child's needs, there can be no substitute for detailed observation and accurate recording of what is seen and heard. Over time, this will confirm how the child is changing and moving on to later stages of development.

Understanding grammar

Studies of child language development (e.g. Brown 1973; Wells 1985) suggest that children go through stages when they develop understanding of different aspects of the structure – grammar – of language. The development of the grammar of words, morphology, such as plurality, tenses and prepositions, seems to be linked with similar co-occurring cognitive and conceptual features. In formal 'test' procedures of understanding of language the procedure often assesses both the language and the cognitive and conceptual associations. Moreover, cognitive and conceptual associations are heavily influenced by cultural factors. For example, when a doll is placed near a toy bed, children have been observed to put the doll in the bed, whether or not they are instructed to. In the UK, many people put spoons into teacups to stir the milk and sugar into the tea and the association between spoons and cups would be automatic for them. However, in other countries, such as in the Indian subcontinent, tea is made differently and spoons are not necessary, so that children from these communities would not automatically associate that spoons go into cups. The implications for assessing understanding of language is that we need to be aware that we may be assessing more abilities and knowledge than just language.

In coming to understand grammatical structure of utterances children seem to adopt several strategies (Precious and Conti-Ramsden 1988). Some children pass through these strategies so quickly that the phase is barely discernible, while other children may continue to use each strategy for some time. Children with difficulties understanding grammatical structure often continue to use one strategy rather than move on to a more adult-like way of understanding grammatical structures. Various strategies have been identified in studies of children's language development: child-centred, word order, plausibility or probable event, intermediate and adult-like.

Child-centred strategy of understanding places the listener-child as the actor of the action. It seems to be the earliest way of understanding. It is in line with Piagetian and other cognitivists' ideas about egocentric perceptions in early development. Using this strategy the child may understand the utterance:

The baby kisses the dolly   as   I kiss the dolly.

Word Order strategy: Children may develop a strategy based on the word order of the utterance, interpreting the noun-verb-noun sequence as actor-action object. This works well for 'active' structures but reverses the meaning for 'passive' structures. Children understanding language according to word order strategy would interpret these two sentences as different:

(i) *The snake ate the rat* (active): understood as 'snake ate rat'
(ii) *The rat was eaten by the snake* (passive): understood as 'rat ate snake'.

The other grammatical information in sentence (ii) which informs us that the snake was the actor is not understood, and is ignored, by children using the word order strategy.

Children move on from using the word order strategy. It has been suggested that they begin to perceive the other morphological aspects of the utterance, such as *was* and *by* and begin to differentiate their understanding (White 1987). Alternatively, they may perceive that in some utterances the vocabulary does not permit a word order strategy.

Plausibility or probable event strategy usually develops following the word order strategy, where the child supports grammatical understanding with knowledge of the world. For example, compare these two utterances:

(i) The daddy carried the baby.
(ii) The baby was carried by the daddy.

Understanding utterance (ii) with a word order strategy would challenge children's knowledge of the world, because they know that babies cannot carry daddies. They must find an alternative interpretation which is based on plausibility or probable event.

An **intermediate** stage may be identified in some children's understanding of grammar where they use several strategies inconsistently, before developing adult-like understanding of structure. By using strategies which depend on taking into account grammatical and vocabulary information, and knowledge of the world, children develop adult-like understanding of utterances. As adults, when we encounter an utterance which we find we cannot understand immediately, we may fall back on strategies which involve trying out various grammatical constructions on the utterance. For example, what is the meaning of the following utterance if heard at a birthday party?

The girl passed the parcel passed the parcel.

A word order strategy would ignore the last three-word phrase and interpret the structure as an actor-action-object structure. We could make this interpretation plausible by suggesting that if it were a spoken utterance the speaker was repeating the last phrase for emphasis. However, these strategies do not understand the grammar of the utterance. We need to impose a relative clause structure on this utterance in order to make its structure clear.

The girl, who had been passed the parcel, passed the parcel.

This example shows that adult grammatical knowledge enables us to move away from a word-by-word interpretation of structure and seek more complex structures. Adult knowledge of grammar understands that grammatical structure is not linear but hierarchical. Structures can be embedded within each other, and there can be several structures, clauses or phrases, within one utterance. For example:

The lion, having eaten the bones from the hunter's camp,
climbed the tree to be out of the sun.

Other examples of hierarchical structure in utterance are formed by words which signal to us to hold the first piece of information because understanding subsequent information is dependent on it. Words such as *since, not only/but also, before, after*; such as in these examples:

(i) Since it's raining outside you will have to play in the hall.
(ii) Not only must you wash your hands but you must comb your hair too.
(iii) Before you line up, put your books away.
(iv) After you have put your books away, line up.

Processing these utterances requires that children recognise the grammatical structure of these words and the utterance. They must process the parts of the utterance through storage and retrieval. Presenting the parts of the utterances in the order in which they will take place helps to interpret them. Examples (iii) and (iv) illustrate this most clearly. Using the words *before* and *after* in this way can be confusing for many children, and it may be useful to use alternatives such as *first* and *and then* with children who have particular difficulties processing these structures. Some children may have difficulties retrieving the first part of the utterance and process, and act on, only the last part. With these children it may be necessary to use only single structure sentences while they develop their language processing skills with a support and intervention programme.

It has been suggested that difficulty in processing utterances with several structures is due to the child's restricted short-term auditory memory. However, this may not always be the case. There are studies which point out that difficulties in interpreting complex utterances are more likely to be due to the child's difficulty processing the complexity of the hierarchical nature of the grammar. This has been shown by children correctly understanding utterances which are longer, that is have more words, but have simple structures (Cromer 1991; Foster 1990).

Recent studies (Evans 2002) in grammatical understanding find that children with language difficulties are likely to show different use of comprehension strategies than their typically developing peers. Their comprehension difficulties seem to be due to the children's limitations in processing capacity which have an impact on shaping, or failing to shape, the underlying representations of language grammatical information. Furthermore, their comprehension is also highly vulnerable to increases in external, contextual processing demands which results in variable performances of understanding. There are implications for assessment, as well as for teaching and intervention. Identifying points of instability in comprehension in a pupil can lead teachers and others to controlling changes in contextual demands and improving performance in language comprehension.

Comprehension and curriculum

The effects on pupils' learning of difficulties in paying attention, listening and understanding are easy to imagine. On entry to school, pupils are expected to listen and learn in a variety of ways which may be particularly challenging for some. In a large group, information or instructions may be given at a speed which is appropriate for the majority but may leave others confused. Language will be used in new and unfamiliar contexts by adults whose voices and styles of speaking will differ from those the child knows. Staff in nurseries and schools will observe children in a range of activities which will give clues about their level of understanding. Ann Locke and Maggie Beech have developed systematic recording procedures for 'emerging language' skills in the early years. Among the behaviours which indicate skills of listening and understanding they include children's responses to songs and rhymes, responses to stories, simple instructions and the ability to cooperate in games where instructions are given (Locke and Beech 1991).

Further challenges to comprehension are presented on transition from primary to secondary schooling where there may be considerable changes in the style of teaching. It has been suggested that in secondary schools, teachers spend less time with individuals and small groups (Galton and Willocks 1983). Language is an essential element of the teaching and learning of any subject and in secondary school, pupils will encounter a larger number of teachers, each with their own style and with a language for their own subject. Additionally, there are increased demands on pupils' understanding of written language when they are expected to read in order to learn a subject.

First, consider how the language used in different curriculum areas may make particular demands on a pupil's comprehension. Key elements of the understanding of history, for example, include understanding of words and phrases relating to the passing of time: before, after, a long time ago, past (Department for Education and Employment and Qualifications and Curriculum Authority 1999: 104). In science, understanding of 'scientific vocabulary' is necessary to describe 'living things, materials and their properties and physical processes' (p.78). The mathematics curriculum at Key Stage 2 (Age 7–11) states that pupils should be taught to 'understand and investigate general statements' (for example, 'there are four prime numbers less than 10'; 'wrist size is half neck size') (p.67).

Consider for a moment the implications of these statements for pupils who have difficulties in understanding language. Daniels and Anghileri (1995) suggest that there are differences in meaning between 'Ordinary English' and 'Mathematical English' . For example, some words will have the same meaning in Mathematical and in Ordinary English, for example *because* and *cat*, but other words will have specific mathematical meaning, for example, *parallelogram* and *coefficient*. Yet other words will have a meaning when used mathematically which is different from their sense in ordinary usage. Daniels and Anghileri give as an example the word *odd* which in mathematics may refer to the characteristics of numbers and in ordinary English may mean strange or unusual.

There may be particular difficulties for pupils who have not mastered comparatives: *bigger than* or *greater than*; some pupils may have difficulties in understanding instructions in a sequential pattern: 'Add three and seven, then take away the sum of two and four'. Further, many mathematical problems are 'made real' by contextualising them in situations and stories which pupils are expected to find meaningful. For pupils who have difficulties in comprehending language, this may present particular problems and may, in fact, obscure the mathematical tasks for them.

For example, in a mathematics test for 13–14-year-olds, pupils were asked to sort animals into groups. This is essentially a non-verbal categorisation task. However, the animals were given arbitrary human names, such as Sally, Huw, Razak. This redundant information would have overloaded the processing abilities of children with difficulties understanding language (Martin *et al.* 1992). Pupils who are experiencing difficulties in acquiring understanding of word meanings may find any of these aspects of the subject difficult and similar problems may arise in each curriculum subject.

The classroom environment

There are two levels on which children may appear to have difficulties. The first is at the level of auditory acuity or perception. Pupils who have difficulties in listening and attention may be disadvantaged if they fail to hear or perceive the differences between similar sounding words such as between sixteen and sixty or forty and fourteen. As well as the mathematical difficulties this might cause, simple instructions such as 'Turn to page. . .' would be problematic. Straightforward strategies to support these pupils would be to ensure that they sat near the teacher, that the teacher checked that they had understood the instruction and that written information was also provided if appropriate.

On another level, some pupils may appear not to be able to follow discussion in the classroom. One explanation could be along cognitive lines, that they are unable to appreciate the abstract, hypothetical ideas which are part of some discussions. However, the discussions in the classroom may not be at such an abstract level and still these pupils may not be able to follow them. Interestingly, they may be able to demonstrate that they are able to understand the cognitive and conceptual basis of the discussion in a one-to-one conversation with the teacher. This may be explained by the suggestion that these pupils process language at a slower pace than their peers (Bamford and Saunders 1985). We have noted in Chapter 6 that some children may need more time to respond successfully to the teacher's questions. These pupils may have a mild *central auditory processing difficulty*. Some individual support may be appropriate for these pupils, for example, to go through material following a lesson in order to ensure their understanding. It would be important to note the specific aspects of language which the pupil had found difficult.

Understanding in literacy

We have mentioned above that much of pupils' learning in school rests heavily on literacy, as with reading from the blackboard, worksheets and text-books, and this is the case for many pupils from junior school (eight years) onwards. Different texts make varying demands on children's language abilities in terms of understanding grammar and vocabulary and it seems that young people continue to develop their language through reading and writing (Perera 1986). We have discussed the fact that children's understanding of spoken utterances improves when the items of information are put in the sequence in which they occur. Similarly, in understanding reading texts, Perera (1992) argues that chronologically organised texts are easier to interpret at the level of the relationship between sentences, paragraphs and chapters because temporal sequence is a familiar and generally straightforward concept (p.187).

In the same way, children find it easier to organise their written work in chronological sequence. In texts which are not chronologically organised, such as this one, writers may try to point out relations, such as similarity, cause-effect, contrast, by using connectives, like 'by the same token', 'therefore', 'alternatively'. Studies of understanding of non-chronological text reveal that pupils up to 15 years old who have no language difficulties find these connectives difficult (Robertson 1968; Gardner 1977; Henderson 1979 cited in Perera 1992).

In the classroom we can support understanding of language in literacy by encouraging pupils to identify the sequence in what they read and in what they write. Where material in texts or worksheets is not chronologically organised we can encourage pupils to develop strategies to identify the parts of the text which refer to the same topic or aspect of the topic, by writing in subheadings or by using colour coding. Activities which allow pupils to work together on this can be rewarding. For example, discussing what elements do go together and what the subheading might be; encouraging them to notice the headings and the layout of the paragraphs as well as the sentences and the use of connectives. Pupils can be encouraged to use and adapt these strategies in their writing.

It is worth remembering that the curriculum should encourage pupils to read a wide variety of texts and this was the recommendation of the Report of the English Working Group (DES 1989). Children need to be prepared for the demands on literacy in everyday life as well as for the demands of education, by being able to read not only labels, letters, notices, comics and tabloid newspapers but also subject textbooks and journals. We can use the strategies of literacy across a range of texts.

Assessment

It is much easier to assess an individual's expressive language than their receptive language. The usual way we test receptive language is to offer tasks to which the person must respond depending on their understanding the verbal instruction. The person should not have to say anything. Such tasks comprise pointing to a named picture from a small selection which has been chosen because they are all similar in linguistic terms. The child may be asked to manipulate small toys in response to instructions. There are assessment procedures which investigate these stages and aspects of development of understanding language, some of which we have mentioned in previous chapters, and we pinpoint a few more now.

Children's ability to interpret utterances by the word order strategy can be investigated by procedures such as the *Derbyshire Rapid Screening Test* (Knowles and Masidlover 1987). This test looks at whether the child can understand the Information Carrying Words (ICWs) in an utterance, rather than the grammatical morphemes. Similarly much of the comprehension scale of the *Reynell Developmental Language Scales* (Edwards *et al.* 1997) applies to word order strategy and key information words, such as colour and size. Both of these procedures may be familiar to practitioners in classrooms. It is important to appreciate the stage and aspect of understanding language they investigate and that they are not primarily assessing grammatical structure.

There are other assessments which look more at the structure of early emerging grammatical forms, such as the *Northwestern Syntax Screening Test* (Lee 1971) which is North American and the *Revised Sentence Comprehension Test* (Wheldall *et al.* 1987) which is from the UK. This procedure investigates the child's interpretation of grammatical structures across both English and Panjabi. There are also assessment procedures which investigate the ability to process and interpret complex grammatical structures, for example the *Test for Reception Of Grammar* (TROG) (Bishop 1983).

Most of these assessment procedures are available only in English. How do we assess the understanding of language in bilingual pupils?

Assessing understanding in bilingual children

There are certain issues which need to be considered when investigating the understanding of language in children who are developing bilingually and who come from linguistic minority communities. We mentioned earlier the cultural influences which can help or hinder a child's understanding of language. In fact the relationship between culture and language is one of dependence, according to some (Halliday 1973). Language is the vehicle of culture; we learn our values, belief systems and relationships through language. Thus, suggestions to separate language from culture in assessment procedures seem seriously flawed. An alternative approach would be to acknowledge and exploit the relationship to the benefit of the pupils and their learning.

One way forward is to consider developing assessment procedures in the pupil's mother tongue or other languages. This is becoming regular practice among some speech and language therapists and educational psychologists. Assessments in both languages are able to show strengths and weaknesses of the individual in understanding (and also expression). Bilingual profiles are likely to reveal if the difficulty exists in one language only, such as second language English, or whether the pupil has a difficulty in processing and understanding both languages. Among some linguistic minority communities in the UK, such as in Wales, bilingual curriculum assessments are accepted practice.

Some practitioners have translated language assessment procedures from one language, usually English, into another language, usually a linguistic minority community language. Considerable caution and rigour needs to be applied if associated difficulties are to be avoided. Materials in the procedure would need to be made culturally appropriate; selected language structures would need to assess the grammatical, semantic and pragmatic features salient to the language, possibly with a view to their developmental emergence; and the procedure would need to be standardised on the relevant bilingual population group, if appropriate (Duncan 1989).

Observation

Many young children with difficulties understanding language will not be able to cope with formal assessment procedures because they have not yet developed sufficient attention and receptive language to participate. The main source of information about this group of children will come from classroom and home observations, concerning how frequently they respond to language, such as to their name or to instructions; how they respond to language with peers and siblings. Videotaping such children in a language interaction is invaluable. Information about how these children perform in different situations and contexts is important, since studies have shown that contextual demands alter comprehension performance in these children. Observing them in a noisy room or in a quiet place, on their own with a peer or peers or with an adult, in an unstructured situation or in a structured one would yield important information about their language understanding.

Comprehension monitoring

If we suspect that a child or a young person may have difficulties understanding language then what can we do about it? Often these difficulties are sufficiently serious to interrupt the pupil's access to the curriculum. Consequently, extra support and an intervention programme would be indicated. In the classroom, encouraging the child to be 'ready to listen' is a worthwhile support strategy to any intervention programme. Listening behaviours need to be made explicit to this group of children they need to be told and shown how to sit still, how to focus on the speaker how to turn-take. Integral to this, is that they need to be able to model 'good' and 'bad' listening behaviours so that they are focusing on each other and giving each other feedback (Dollaghan 1987).

Other strategies include checking that they are understanding specific vocabulary and the sequence of events in one activity, such as a short story or an aspect of a lesson. Making explicit that you want them to listen and then showing that you are interested in what they have understood brings their need to listen to the foreground. It should also inform us about what information needs to be retraced. For older children one important principle when interacting with them is to encourage them to signal when they are not understanding the language you use. This requires developing considerable personal skills in the pupils which will allow them to be sufficiently assertive with regard to their difficulty.

Behaviour and understanding

Before leaving this discussion of comprehension difficulties, we should mention 'behaviour'. It should by now be easy to see that many of the indications that a child does not understand could also be construed as difficult behaviour. A child who does not pay attention to what, for the teacher, is important, may be a challenge. The child may also distract other children and prevent them from learning. Other signs that the child has not understood could also be interpreted as uncooperative or oppositional behaviour. For example, a child who cannot follow complex instructions may spend a lot of time looking around the classroom or out of the window. They will frequently misunderstand what is required and so will do the wrong thing, or do nothing. Some children will repeat all or part of what has been said to them, perhaps in an attempt to 'play for time' and process what has been said. This can appear rude and insolent. Children who have difficulties in understanding are often forgetful and disorganised. They fail to bring the right equipment to school or they arrive late. They may not understand the rules and routines of the classroom, or indeed, the rules of games with other children so that they encounter difficulties.

While the immediate response may be to focus on the surface behaviour, it will be important to consider whether the behaviour has been misinterpreted. Detailed assessment may show that there are comprehension difficulties and that the child needs help to understand language and to learn alongside their peers.

Conclusion

The area of receptive language is complex and our knowledge is limited. Formal test procedures are not extensive and much more investigation is needed in this field. In practice we rely a great deal on observational information from parents, teachers, therapists, psychologists and others. The importance of this information cannot be exaggerated for comprehension of language is one of the most fundamental keys to learning in school.

Further reading

Bishop, D.V. M. (1997) *Uncommon Understanding: Development and Disorders of Language Comprehension in Children.* Hove: Psychology Press.

Chapter 9

Working in a team

Introduction

The last few chapters have focused on some of the characteristics of language and communication difficulties and on the needs of children who experience these. We have, we hope, made it clear that language as an element of human communication relies on essential interactions and relationships between people. Relationships between people will be a vital element in the planning of help for children in school. In this chapter, the importance of interactive processes characteristic of families and work groups is discussed and emphasis is placed on the role of parents' relationships with professionals. Finally, it is suggested that professionals who work with pupils with language and communication difficulties and advise colleagues about this require special knowledge and skills.

Looking at the system

A family, a school, a community or any other organisation can be looked at as a system in which people interact with each other. All of the members affect and are affected by each other. In a family, each person has significance for each other member and each member contributes to the overall uniqueness of that family. In a school all of the people are important in different ways for others. We only need to look at what happens when a member of staff leaves an organisation, or when someone new is appointed, to see that this often results in general changes and can give rise to a variety of strong feelings in different individuals. A new pupil in a class can make a difference to many of the others. In a family, the effects on children, when, say, a parent is ill or has to go away for some time will often be noticed by changes in behaviour in school. People cannot help but react to each other.

We are all participants in a range of groups and systems, in work, family and social aspects of our lives. Many overlap and interact with each other. Families for example, have contact with school systems. Each class is a subsystem of a school, which is a subsystem of a local education authority We can go on for a long time looking at the larger, local and national systems whose policies and ways of working interact with and influence schools. No individual or group can act independently without some impact on cther members of their own or another group which, in turn affects the way they behave. In working to meet the needs of children with language and communication difficulties, family and school systems also have to interact with other service systems. In the UK, the main providers, apart from the education service, are the health and the social services. There are also private organisations and non-governmental groups or voluntary bcdies which contribute to the provision.

Every group has its own characteristics and ways of operating. These may be determined by explicit rules and structures. There will also be many implicit, unspoken rules and ways of behaving which may have developed over time and will change as different people join or leave the group. Ary of the official and the unspoken rules can enhance or obstruct the effectiveness of the system. In recent years, the UK government has stated a wish to promote 'joined-up thinking' between its departments, giving a 'seamless service'. This is presumably an effort to create more compatible systems which share beliefs and procedures so that more effective services can be provided. We will discuss below some of the characteristics of the services which provide for children with language and communication needs and examine how they may work together.

Policies and guidance

Many countries have developed, or are in the process of developing, policies and guidance on people with disabilities and their inclusion in society. In 1994, a conference of the United Nations' education division produced what has become known as the Salamanca Statement (UNESCO 1994). Representatives of 92 governments, including the UK and 25 international organisations, supported the concept of inclusion of all children in the regular education system, regardless of their physical, intellectual, sccial, emotional, linguistic or other conditions.

Also in 1994, the UK government published a code of practice on the identification and assessment of special educational needs (Department for Education and Employment 1994). This has been revised to become the Special Educational Needs Code of Practice (Department for Education and Skills 2001). Because of devolutionary processes, this applies to England but there are similar documents in other parts of the UK. 'LEAs (Local

Education Authorities), schools, early education settings and those who help them – including health and social services – must have regard to it. They must not ignore it' (p.iii).

There is then, an explicit 'rule' that different services should work together in providing for children with special educational needs. There is an implication of a whole-systems approach because the SEN Code is also explicitly linked with the Code of Practice on Disability Rights (Disability Rights Commission 2001) which prohibits discrimination against disabled people in all aspects of life. Support for children who have special educational needs in language and communication, which potentially interfere with their learning in school may therefore be influenced by several aspects of guidance and policy at a general level which puts responsibility on services to provide for them.

With particular reference to language and communication needs, initiatives were promoted by the UK government's Programme of Action for meeting special educational needs (Department for Education and Employment 1998). This recognised that support for children with these needs had been inadequate for a long time. If more inclusive education was to be promoted, more speech and language therapy (SLT) in schools was necessary. Several research and practical projects were set up in response to the Programme of Action.

Similarities and differences which enhance or obstruct

Statutory responsibility for formal teaching and learning in schools rests with the education service in collaboration with parents. Where children have special educational needs, the education and family systems often have to interact with staff and procedures from health and social services. Children with language and communication needs are most likely to be supported by teachers and speech and language therapists (SLTs). In the UK, the majority of SLTs have been employed by the National Health Service since 1974. Perhaps because therapists were employed by health, school-aged children have often been expected to attend clinics, during school hours, for support for their communication skills from a therapist.

The employment of teachers and speech and language therapists in two different services has often been cited as a major obstacle affecting provision for children. The separation into education and health systems, with different ways of operating, does not help the two professional groups to work together. It has been observed that teachers and therapists have different ways of thinking about language and communication (Miller 1999).

Teachers, who are concerned with the curriculum, focus on children's ability to use language in social settings for thinking and learning with others. Speech and language therapists tend to focus on the detail of the components of language and speech and what influences them, usually with particular respect to an individual child. They will be especially concerned to know 'what is wrong' and why this child communicates in this way. We can link these approaches to the ways of looking at language which were discussed in Chapters 1 and 2 and we would suggest that it is important to combine approaches if the needs of a child are to be met.

There are signs that a combination of approaches is now recognised in official documents. The revised SEN Code of Practice (Department for Education and Skills 2001) unambiguously sees speech and language difficulties as educational needs which must be provided for in an educational setting. '. . . since communication is so fundamental in learning and progression, addressing speech and language impairment should normally be recorded as educational provision unless there are *exceptional* reasons for not doing so' p.105.

Professional Standards for speech and language therapists also require them to provide therapy for children 'as an integral part of their school life' (Royal College of Speech and Language Therapists 1996). The professional body states, in these Standards, that a service to mainstream schools will involve 'a high degree of shared knowledge, skills, expertise and information among all those involved with the child' (p.54). The expectation then, of both the health and education professionals, is that they will work together to provide support for children in an educational context.

What then are the characteristics of the systems in which teachers and speech and language therapists practise which would obstruct or facilitate their work together? Different ways of working are linked with different professional cultures. The beliefs, assumptions and ways of working of the practitioners, linked with structures of the services and terms of employment may create systems which are difficult for outsiders to penetrate and understand. This is very similar to the way in which families have unique characteristics and ways of doing things which can sometimes be difficult for others to understand.

It has been suggested by Norwich (1990) that professions develop and change in response to the changing needs of clients. We can find many examples of this over recent years. Teachers have been responding to initiatives on inclusive education by training to meet special needs in mainstream classrooms. The role of Special Educational Needs Coordinator (SENCO) has become more prominent as all schools have been required to identify a person in this position. Speech and language therapists have, over recent years, taken on responsibility for working with people who develop problems in swallowing (dysphagia). This initially led to a burgeoning of courses to train therapists in this work and finally, it was agreed by the profession that knowledge and skills for dysphagia work should be included in undergraduate courses for SLTs.

Perhaps another, more obvious example of change in the profession is evidenced by the change of name. A few years ago, following a vote by members of the profession, 'speech therapists' became 'speech and language therapists', as they believed that this more accurately reflected their work with language, rather than speech problems. These types of changes however, are also affected by what other professions are offering. In the case of swallowing problems, there were many discussions about whether nurses or other health care workers should be responsible for this. Professions need to maintain differences and distinctions in the special knowledge and skills they can offer and this can sometimes be a source of tension and suspicion between them. A current example of this in the UK is the discussion about the role of teachers with relation to learning support assistants and the distinctions between their responsibilities.

While professions do need to be aware of the specialist services they can offer, it is unproductive to protect these interests to the extent that knowledge and skills are not shared. It is important that professions are concerned more with the needs of their clients than their own self-interest.

A helpful analysis of the systems in which speech and language therapists and teachers work has been made by Elspeth McCartney and her colleagues (McCartney 1999). Using a model developed by Banathy (1973, cited by McCartney 1999) the education and health services are compared from the perspectives of their functions, structures, processes and environment.

The *functions* of health and education are the goals of the service, what they are trying to achieve. Health and education are clearly different in this respect and they may have differences in the way they prioritise children's needs, depending on factors such as severity or urgency and indeed, resources.

At the level of *structure*, the services have different decision-making procedures and ways of organising themselves. The education service for example, mainly educates children in schools, in groups, during set times. The therapy services in health have traditionally worked in clinics, often with individuals and are not constrained by school terms and timetables. Therapists' and teachers' contracts of employment have different requirements.

Processes relate to the behaviour of the system, for example, its procedures for accepting referrals and for enabling children to pass through the service. In schools, an example of this is the staged process of assessment with action at school level or at the level requiring assistance from external agencies. The SLT service has been keen to say that it is available to all children and does not prioritise only those with statements or records of need.

The *environment* of the system is the larger society in which it operates. This relates to local and national communities for example and to the particular groups of people who are its clients. McCartney uses the example of services' interactions with families to compare education and health. Although schools have an obligation to work with parents, it is clearly not possible to accommodate all individual needs and the overriding concern must be for the larger population in a school. The therapy service has normally tried to include parents in work with their children as they support the specific needs of a child. Parents have often come to expect individual attention for their child.

Examining education, health and other services in this way can be helpful in showing how they are similar and different and where their functions, structure, processes and environment may be incompatible, obstructive or facilitative to each other. An analysis of this type could be made on a large scale at national level and could also be applied to local services to look at where changes might be made to enhance collaboration.

Therapists and teachers – beliefs and activities

Having looked at the characteristics of the settings for SLT and teaching, it is appropriate to consider in more detail the knowledge, skills and understanding of the practitioners themselves. We need to consider what is distinctive about a school teacher and about a speech and language therapist.

- What have they been trained to do and how have they been 'brought up' to think?
- What are their strengths and how can they contribute to each other's work?
- In what ways are they similar and how are they different?

Answers to these questions can help us to think what, and how, SLTs and teachers can learn from each other.

Speech and language therapists are trained to help people of all ages who have difficulties with their communication or related problems in feeding and swallowing. Around 75 per cent of therapists in the UK work with children, many of them in the preschool and early years. The SLT will be able to make a detailed assessment of a child's developing speech and language skills because of their training in linguistics and phonetics and human development. A knowledge of neurology, anatomy and physiology as well as psychology will lead them to think about what may be underneath a child's difficulties and whether there are factors within the child which may be interacting with particular features of the child's environment. It is probably true to say that speech and language therapists have usually taken a problem-focused approach, concentrating on the individual. However, there is an increasing interest in group work and social settings for speech and language therapy and many are now seeing schools as appropriate contexts for this.

It is useful to know that, in the UK, anyone may refer themselves or another person to a speech and language therapist. It is not necessary to go first to a doctor. The curriculum followed by speech and language therapists in their professional education has, until recently been guided by the professional body, the Royal College of Speech and Language Therapists (RCSLT). The profession has now become one of the 'Health Care Professions' and is controlled, in conjunction with RCSLT, by a body which requires practitioners to be state registered.

Teachers are trained to develop children's learning through the curriculum and other activities. Much of this learning takes place with others in groups. Most teachers specialise in a particular age group and subject area. For example, in secondary schools it is usual for the teachers to be responsible for particular subjects, such as science, or geography or a modern foreign language. In primary schools, teachers have also usually specialised in a curriculum area, such as English, mathematics or science. They may also be especially experienced with a particular age group and there are some, nursery teachers, who work in nursery schools. They are experienced in the education of children at the preschool level. Professional education for teachers is overseen by agencies working on behalf of the government. In England, the Teacher Training Agency has set out standards for different roles in teaching including, as we shall see later, specialist standards for teachers working with special educational needs, including language and communication needs.

All teachers should have basic knowledge and skills to work with pupils with special educational needs and a few will have specialist training to work with pupils described as having speech or language difficulties. A crucial member of the team is a designated member of staff to look after any arrangements for pupils who may have difficulties with their learning. In the UK, this designated person is the Special Educational Needs Coordinator (SENCO). The SEN Code of Practice (Department for Education and Skills 2001) requires schools to report on the qualifications of these members of staff. As a model of practice, the Code sets out the functions of the Special Educational Needs Coordinator, who is responsible for the day-to-day operation of a school's SEN policy. A key function is to 'develop effective ways of overcoming barriers to learning and sustaining effective teaching through the analysis and assessment of children's needs, by monitoring the quality of teaching and standards of pupils' achievements and by setting targets for improvement' (p.50).

In a number of ways therefore, the SENCO will be involved with pupils described as having speech or language needs. Teacher colleagues can expect the SENCO to guide them and to oversee their work with children who experience difficulties.

Learning support assistants in the UK may work as assistants to teachers or they may be allocated to work with a child or a few children who need special help to learn in school. Many of them in the UK will have completed a qualification of the Nursery Nurses Examination Board although increasing numbers now undertake training organised by education authorities leading to National Vocational Qualifications. Speech and language therapists may also work with assistants who will take on some specific tasks with children who need support for their language and communication.

If we were to summarise the professional knowledge and skills of teachers, we could say that their competence is in planning and organising teaching and learning for groups of children. Some teachers will do this with reference to particular aspects of the curriculum and some with children with particular characteristics, of age or learning needs. We could go further and say that for all teachers, the main 'tool' that they use is language. Language is used for teaching and learning, by teachers and by children. Effective teaching and learning in schools successfully combines the language of the children, the adults and the curriculum. Language and communication skills are used in school to form relationships, to inform, respond, direct, question, perform and for a number of other functions.

Speech and language therapists, too, use language as their main professional tool. As we have already suggested, they tend to look at the detail of language by focusing on its components, for example, sounds and grammatical structures or word meanings. They are also concerned with what is going on behind the language. For example, they will ask whether a person can hear, whether they can organise movements to produce sounds using their tongue and lips and whether they have the level of conceptual development to make sense of what others say or to make sense themselves. In making decisions about how to support an individual, SLTs will usually consider the social network of the family, taking account of parents' or partner's reactions and ways of communicating.

Perhaps the greatest similarity between teachers and SLTs is in their use of language as a tool of their trade. However, the two groups of practitioners appear to have a different perspective on language and communication skills. We can describe the teachers' focus as one which emphasises overall performance in communication for teaching and learning. SLTs are more focused on the detail and the individual's ability to make use of the components of language for understanding and expression. Teachers work largely in a context of groups talking and interacting together. Therapists often work with individuals and are concerned with the effectiveness of their communication skills.

These two perspectives on language are complementary and necessary if children with speech and language difficulties are to learn effectively in school. Teachers, mindful of the demands of the curriculum, probably need to understand more about components of language and language difficulties and how they may take account of these in organising classroom tasks. SLTs, who are concerned with language difficulties of individual children, need to understand how schools work and what is required in the curriculum. Therapists and teachers together can plan activities which use and promote language in a classroom setting as part of daily classroom routines. Modification of the classroom environment, effected by changing adults' language and the language of curriculum activities, will be important for engaging children with varied needs in learning. Importantly, although primarily aiming to help children with particular language needs, differentiated language will also benefit their classmates. There will be many children who, while not having identified difficulties, will learn more easily from strategies such as slower speech, repetition, simplification or elaboration of instructions.

Collaboration between different professional groups will not take place unless it is acknowledged that changes are needed. Work as described above means that SLTs must go into schools and must be accommodated in classrooms. For teachers and SLTs to focus on particular children and to plan for their needs together, time must be set aside. There is an increasing amount of research which has identified this as a key factor in professional collaboration. In the specific context of work with pupils with speech and language difficulties, Jannet Wright (1992) looked at the working practices of teachers and speech-language therapists who worked together. She found that the most successful collaboration occurred where therapists went into schools and had timetabled sessions for discussion with teachers. Both professions expressed satisfaction with this arrangement and reported how much they learned from each other. It does not take an enormous leap of the imagination to believe that these professionals probably worked more effectively with the children.

Lacey (2001) also identified time as a general problem for teams of teachers and different types of therapists in a special school. Almost all of the people she interviewed had negative things to say about the lack of time to work and talk to each other. She ascribes this to the different ways in which therapists and teachers traditionally structure their time. Teachers work in blocks of time and therapists, she believes, work down lists of people, one-by-one. If this is so, or if there are other reasons for the limited time, compromises will be necessary if teachers and therapists are to find common time to get together. Classrooms are busy places and the priority is the children's learning. Discussion between the adults must take place outside lesson time. This means that official recognition of the need for time must be given by senior managers. Head teachers and SENCOs will need to provide time for teachers and SLTs' employers will need to accept that time for discussion is as legitimate as working one-to-one with children.

Parents and professionals

So far, we have said little about the part played by parents in the team with professionals but it is important to know that there are now 'rules' that parents should be treated as partners in work with children with special educational needs. The system is characterised by professionals who 'actively seek to work with parents and value the contribution they make' (Department for Education and Skills 2001 2.1).

For most children in the early years, the home has the most powerful influence on their development. Language development is no exception and, for the majority, early language is learned at home. Most teachers are aware of the research finding that the experiences of language children had in the nursery were rather limited by comparison with the rich variety of language they were involved in at home (Tizard and Hughes 1984). By the time a child goes to school, if language development has gone well, they are ready to take advantage of a wide range of new opportunities. They do this by responding to new adults and children and by speaking for themselves in a wide variety of situations. Their home and family has provided them with useful tools for learning, including language and communication skills.

We know, from research undertaken with families, that most parents are very aware of their children's development. Many parents have been able to identify communication problems by the time their child is two years old (AFASIC 1993). They do this in several ways. Parents who have more than one child compare their children's development; they compare their children with those outside the family; they hear comments from other family members and friends; perhaps, though, most obviously, because they know their child very well, they are very quick to spot when something is not right.

Not surprisingly, parents who think that there may be something different about their child may begin to worry. This may not be helped if they seek advice and are told, by professionals, not to worry. It is not uncommon for parents to be told, that their child 'will grow out of it' when they seem to be later to develop than other children. In the early stages, it is often very difficult to be certain that a child will grow out of a communication difficulty, because, as we noted in Chapter 2, unless we watch the *pattern* of development, over a period of time, it is not usually possible to predict what will happen. It is therefore always important to take seriously parents' concerns about their children and to take time over deciding whether there are likely to be genuine longer-term worries or whether their anxieties can be helped more immediately.

Characteristics of families

Families, like other social groups, have their own characteristics and structure. As an obvious feature, some families are larger than others. You are probably familiar with the terms 'extended' family and 'nuclear' family, to describe the structures of families. The terms relate not only to the size of the families but, for example, to the relationships within them, to the decision-making processes and the arrangements for care of children.

The structures and relationships in families will be relevant to how they respond to events and to changes in their circumstances. In the same way that individuals go through a life cycle with events which cause them stress, happiness, or sadness, so do families. The idea behind a family life cycle is that a family needs to adjust and develop as it responds to changes in its members, who are themselves passing through developmental stages. It becomes easier to understand this concept when we consider how families deal with major events such as deaths, illnesses or children leaving home. Consider families that you know and how differently they behave. Adjusting to events takes time and this will partly be dependent on the responses of individual members who will affect the reactions of the family as a group.

We discuss these issues because professionals can sometimes react strongly to the behaviour of parents or other family members when a child in school is said to have a difficulty. We need to keep in mind the fact that their understanding of a situation will be different from our own, that they have different priorities. We will not be aware of all of the nuances and characteristics of the relationships between family members or of all recent events in their lives. However, the more we can try to understand how they see the world, the more possibilities there will be that we can work in collaboration with them.

The knowledge parents have of their child is vitally important to school staff and if a child is experiencing difficulties, say with their speech, which may be interfering with their learning, it will be essential for the parents and teachers to have a full discussion on how they are going to work together. This type of working partnership may not be easy at first. Parents may not be clear about how they can help and school staff may not feel confident in communicating with adults. They are, after all, trained to work with children. People's memories and experiences of their own schooldays and of how they felt when their parents visited school may colour their present feelings. It is not so long ago that parents only went into schools on 'parents' evenings', perhaps for a rather formal interview with a teacher. Teachers could not have gained much experience in communicating with parents and parents probably did not learn much about how schools work. It may be useful to think a little more about the relationships between parents and school staff. The following activity may help.

Meeting parents

If you work with children and their parents, it may be helpful to take a look at the circumstances of your meetings.

Think of a child whose parents you have seen in the past.
Where did you see them?
Was the meeting prearranged?

A prearranged meeting allows both parties to think ahead and plan a meeting. If the parent asks to see you as you are rushing out of school or as you are involved with someone else in the playground, it is unlikely that you will be able to give them your best attention. If you are able to plan ahead, you should be able to find somewhere to meet where you will not be disturbed.

The time and place where we meet with a person can give an indication of how much importance we place on them and on the conversation. A conversation, which, for example, takes place in the corridor, within earshot of everyone else, is likely to be different from one which takes place in a quiet, comfortable room with no one else around. The time available is likely to affect what is said and it is important that the amount of time is always made clear at the outset. Such boundaries of time and place can strongly influence the success or otherwise of a meeting. Think of the times when you have 'got stuck' with someone who 'just would not stop talking'. Were there any indications from either of you that the conversation would be limited? Of course, in conversations with friends, this is often not necessary, and it is part of their pleasure, but here we are talking about working relationships, which are essentially different.

An analysis such as that suggested above may indicate that the interview has not really achieved very much and it may be helpful to consider the following questions after the meeting.

Who did most of the talking? The communicative behaviour of one of the individuals may have meant that the other did very little talking. If the professional did most of the talking, the parent may not have had an opportunity to say much. If the parent(s) talked a lot, the professional may not have known how to stop them and to maintain the purpose of the interview.

The parent(s) may have been very reserved and the professional may not have known how to help them to 'open up'. Many parents, when they visit schools, feel nervous and anxious. Their anxiety may be displayed in a variety of ways: anger, lack of cooperation, difficulty in expressing themselves, hesitancy, as well as nervous mannerisms revealed by their body language. It may be particularly difficult for less articulate parents or for those from ethnic and linguistic minorities for whom a school may represent key aspects of the 'establishment' and authority. You, the professional, are on your own territory, which makes it comfortable for you but which may leave the parent feeling ill at ease. It is up to you to make the parent feel relaxed. You may need to consider whether school is the best place for a meeting – perhaps their home may be better. Additionally, you may need to consider whether the support of a bilingual education worker would help.

By spending a few moments thinking beforehand, you may be assured of a more fruitful meeting. Think of a parent you are in contact with at present, or one that you are going to see in the near future. Before you see them, you might consider the following:

Do you have past experience of this parent which affects your feelings about them?
How do you feel about their son or daughter?
What do you think the parent hopes to gain from the meeting?
What are their main concerns about their child?

You could carry out this brief exercise each time you arrange to see a parent.

Afterwards you should go through each point making comments on your reactions. You should also try to summarise what the parents got out of the meeting and what you got out of the meeting. Did you and the parents go away satisfied? If not, what could have been different?

It is important too, to consider our personal style and our expectations when working with others. To some extent it will be different in every case, depending on the particular nature of the relationship with the other people concerned. On the other hand, we can go into relationships and meetings using the same approach every time. For example, when working with parents, do you always feel it is your duty to give them ideas and suggestions on how to help their child? Or do you think that it is better to let them work out their own way of doing things, for example of teaching their child to read? Some professionals feel strongly that parents should not be expected to teach their children. Others consider that parents can be effective teachers and should be involved. What are your views on all of this? If you are a parent or if you have contact with any children outside of your working life, what would you do?

There are times when parents may request guidance on how to do something to help their child and the professional may have information or skills which may be useful. After all, people would not be able to call themselves professionals if they did not have a particular area of knowledge or set of skills which was 'specialised'. However, the same will be true of parents. They may be able to advise professionals on how to get the best from their son or daughter and may transplant some of their skills to the professional practitioner. There are many occasions too, when it would be most appropriate for parents and professionals to discuss the needs of a child and to agree together on a course of action. Individuals vary enormously and will need differing approaches. The particular philosophy of a school will influence modes of working. The importance of identifying these approaches is to become aware of preferred ways of working and why these have been chosen. Before deciding on what can be done to help a particular child and the family, the professional must consider their own and that family's individual characteristics and consider what might be a suitable approach for all concerned. Whatever approach is chosen, it is important that it is adopted for a good reason and not simply out of habit.

Working together

You might try some exercises similar to those above next time you need to discuss a child with a colleague. For example, you will need to ask the following questions if you are to get the most out of your meeting:

- Where will you meet?
- Will you set aside time for the meeting?
- Will you both know beforehand what the meeting will be about?
- During the meeting, will you both understand each other's terminology, for example, do you both understand the same things by such words as 'language', 'speech', 'curriculum'?

Asking ourselves questions about how we work together and how we plan meetings with colleagues can contribute to our effectiveness. If we take time to review a meeting we become more aware of how we can improve our skills and become more efficient practitioners. It also means that we stand to make best use of our time, which, as we all know, is very precious.

Ways of working with speech and language difficulties

It was noted earlier that most children who appear to have early difficulties, perhaps because they start to talk later than their peers, go on to make good progress and catch up with the others. Even when a child continues to have difficulties, and perhaps to need extra help, it will be possible for the child to be educated in an ordinary school. Parents and professionals are increasingly aware of the benefits of children being with their neighbourhood friends and for them to take advantage of all that their local school has to offer. If a child has continuing difficulties with spoken or written language, help may be organised in different ways.

The child's class teacher will help the child, by ensuring that all instructions are understood and that everyone, children and adults, knows how to communicate with the child. The child with a language difficulty will need to be encouraged to use strategies to ensure that they do not miss out on vital information exchanges. For example, the child may be taught to ask questions if they are not completely clear what is required of them. They may be taught 'repair' strategies to clarify what they have said if others do not appear to understand. Classroom activities may need small modifications so that a particular child gets extra practice with some skills. Classroom groupings may be specially planned so that children's particular strengths are used and their weaknesses are minimised. Pupils can learn to help each other in their learning. For example, paired reading schemes ensure that children who need extra help in learning to read are assisted by others who are more advanced (Beard and Oakhill 1994). Each child gains something from the experience. Parents too, are sometimes encouraged into classrooms to help children with specific tasks.

If a child has been referred to a speech and language therapist, then it is essential that the teacher and the therapist collaborate closely. The child's work with the therapist must be linked with curriculum activities in school. The therapist and the teacher must be aware of each other's current aims for the pupil and should set time aside to discuss them. Many speech and language therapists like to see a child for individual help, sometimes on a weekly basis over a period of time. There can be difficulties in this way of working if the therapist cannot go to the child's school.

If the session can take place at the school there are obviously better opportunities for the therapist to communicate with the classroom teacher. Collaboration between the teacher and therapist can ensure that the activities devised to assist particular speech or language difficulties can be linked to work in the curriculum. Teachers and therapists need to be more insistent on the need to work together and on the need to have time allocated for discussion together. Time should not be 'stolen' from the lunch break or between classes in the corridor. This diminishes the importance of collaborative discussions.

Pupils who have more severe communication difficulties may attend a language unit or a language resource base. These special classes are usually based in ordinary schools for the special purpose of providing for the needs of pupils with language difficulties. The classes will be organised in different ways in different education authorities but they should be staffed by teachers who have a special interest in language. In some cases, the teachers will have undertaken a special course in language difficulties. Some of these specialist classes will have a full-time or part-time speech-language therapist appointed to them and in these cases, therapists and teachers will work closely together assessing children's needs and jointly planning learning activities.

A small minority of children with language difficulties will be educated in residential or day schools catering solely for such pupils. It is considered that for these children, highly specialised, intensive teaching and therapy, away from the mainstream of education, can be the best route through all or part of their schooling. There is no doubt that a great deal of expertise can be assembled in such schools and it is clear that some pupils do have profound communication problems which need to be given priority if they are to have access to the school curriculum. However, decisions to send children into such specialised settings are never straightforward. Parents and professionals have to consider the advantages and disadvantages of the length of the journey to the school, whether the child is to be residential and how the child will link with friends and neighbours in their local community.

Additionally, there will be very complex decisions to be made about the language and curriculum opportunities available. Professionals will need to be certain that these are broad, balanced and relevant to the pupils' needs and abilities.

The skills of the professionals

Whenever the education of a child with a speech or language difficulty is under consideration, it will be important to look at what the classroom has to offer in terms of staff skills. Today, all teachers are considered, to some extent, to be teachers of pupils with special educational needs and must expect to teach groups of children with a wide range of abilities. However, if there are children with significant language and communication needs, both teachers and speech and language therapists may have to consider their own needs for further professional development.

Earlier we mentioned the professional standards expected of speech and language therapists working in schools. These are identified for work in mainstream schools, special schools and for special classes. The standards concur strongly with the SEN Code of Practice and state that therapy must be provided 'as an integral part of a child's school life'. The service has to be provided 'in the context of the broad curriculum'. In order to work in this way, therapists may identify additional learning needs for themselves if they have no experience of working in classrooms.

Similarly, teachers who find themselves working with children with language and communication needs may identify gaps in their own knowledge and understanding and may need to seek further professional development. The Teacher Training Agency in England (1999) has identified standards of knowledge, understanding and skills for teachers working with children with difficulties in communication and interaction. In many ways, these represent the areas discussed above requiring teachers to be able to take account of the children's language and to plan the language of the curriculum and their own language so that all three aspects are integrated together.

The need for professional collaboration between SLTs and teachers has been taken very seriously recently and the government has supported the development of a Joint Professional Development Framework (I CAN 2001). The purpose of this was to encourage multi-agency working towards inclusive education by developing knowledge and skills of professionals. The document identifies areas of understanding and practical skills to enable speech and language therapists and teachers to support children with speech, language and communication needs. The Framework sets out three different levels of competence for practitioners according to their roles and responsibilities. At Foundation level for example, practitioners will have broad knowledge of language development and difficulties within educational settings. The Core level would be expected of more specialised teachers and therapists. It identifies detailed aspects of provision for special educational needs and, in particular, for children with language and communication needs. An Extension level is described for more advanced work, perhaps when practitioners are involved in policy-making or in practice-based research.

The value of the Joint Professional Development is that it can provide an audit against which practitioners can check how they are doing and whether they have the skills and understanding for their collaborative work. Evidence that they are competent in this respect will be shown by the outcomes of activities performed jointly by speech and language therapist and teacher.

Conclusion

In this chapter we have discussed collaborative practice to support children described as having speech and language difficulties and needs. It was suggested that special efforts have to be made if people are to work effectively together. Parents and professionals have different needs and expectations and it will be necessary to prepare carefully for collaborative work. In order to do this, we suggested that members of the team require specialist skills and knowledge.

In the next chapter we will look at some examples of practice in classrooms where there are children with particular difficulties in learning through language.

Further reading

I CAN (2001) *Joint Professional Development Framework*. London: I CAN.

McCartney, E. (ed.) (1999) *Speech/Language Therapists and Teachers Working Together: a Systems Approach to Collaboration*. London: Whurr.

Wright, J. and Kersner, M. (1998) *Supporting Children with Communication Problems: Sharing the Workload*. London: David Fulton Publishers.

Chapter 10

Reflecting on practice

Introduction

In this chapter, we introduce the idea of practitioners as investigators and researchers in their work with children with language and communication difficulties. We suggest some ways in which they may seek and record further information about the children and ways in which they may plan activities for the children. The principles on which the examples are based are those which inform good practice with any pupils in school. However, the suggestions focus particularly on language and communication so they will be especially useful for the identification and management of children who may have particular language and communication needs.

What do the children need?

There can be little argument with the view that all children have a right of access to the same community as everyone else and educationally, have the right to a broad and balanced curriculum. For many children, their own interactions with caring people of all ages in their families and schools enables this to happen. However, for some children, the provision of interesting and stimulating opportunities is not enough. For a number of reasons, children may be unable to take advantage of opportunities offered. When children have special needs in speech or language, particular care and imagination will be needed to ensure that they are given appropriate opportunities and that they are able to benefit from them. Anyone dealing with such a child will need particular knowledge of the characteristics of the child's communication skills. They must also consider how the child's communication skills are affected by other people and activities in the world around them.

From other chapters in this book, it should have become apparent that some children have a particular difficulty in learning to talk or learning to understand. Simply encouraging them or 'stimulating' them will not help, indeed, it may confuse them. In a similar way, if a child has particular difficulty in learning to read and write, that is with literacy, it will not be helpful to just provide them with a lot of books. The child's abilities and difficulties need to be examined in detail. Activities planned for the child also need to be considered carefully with special reference to the language involved. If activities can be well matched to the child's interests and abilities, then there is more possibility that they will make progress.

The adults around the child need to have well-developed observation skills and they need to know what to observe. Observation of children with speech or language difficulties means not only looking carefully at what they do but also, listening carefully to what they say and how they say it. The adults need to become investigators.

How can adults help?

Many practitioners do not consider themselves to be researchers but evaluation of practice, careful assessment and observation are all activities familiar to teachers and constitute a form of research. Research can be defined as 'systematic investigation' which is usually then written up for others to read. In this chapter, the idea of practitioners as researchers is put forward in the hope that this will help teachers and others in their work with all children and may also encourage them to contribute valuable experience to practice for children with speech or language difficulties.

First, think of how you go about planning to work with any child or group of children. Although you may not write everything down, you probably go through a process of thinking about what you will do, based on what you know about the child, what you want to achieve and the resources you have available. When you carry out a session based on your ideas, you may have to make rapid decisions to modify your plans according to what actually happens. After the session you probably think about what you did and what the children did and you may think that the session went well or that if you had done something differently, it could have been better. The process of planning, reflecting, acting on the plan and then recording and evaluating the outcomes is an important part of the day-to-day work of teachers and others who work with children. It is also a process which can contribute a great deal to our knowledge of work in educational and social settings. It is the basis of what is sometimes known as practitioner research

Often too, a report has to be written and it is then important to be precise and unambiguous so that others can use the information. If you are asked to write a report on a child, it is helpful to have a format which can be used as a guide.

The same format can be used for different children and for the same child if a further report is required later. The use of the same format, under headings, makes it easier to decide whether there has been any change say, in a child's use of language, since the last report. It means too that if necessary, children can be compared with each other so that it will be easier to see if some children need more help in some aspects of their development than others. Finally, if the same format is used each time, it can save work.

Reporting on children's language

In order to have as much detail as possible for a report on a child's speech and language abilities, it is helpful if several people can comment on the child's communication from a variety of observations in different contexts. So for example, parents will see their child's communication differently from the teacher and the speech and language therapist and all of these people will make important contributions to the overall picture. The more this information is shared, the more it will be possible to use it to help the child. Below is a format which could be used by anyone reporting on a child's communication skills. By using the headings as a guide, it should be possible to highlight any aspects which give rise for concern and may need further investigation.

Observation of a child's communication skills

Preliminary factual information should include the child's name, the name of the person making the observation and the date and place of the observation.

Background information

This should give the child's date of birth, age in years and months and a general brief outline of developmental levels in terms of the child's motor skills, ability to see, to hear and their play interests. This section should state whether there are any concerns about any aspects of the child's development.

Communication

For all of the communication described, information should be given about the context of the information, that is, when and where the event took place and who was present.

Wherever possible, give specific examples of the child's communication and what was said or done by other children or adults who were involved, written down as accurately as possible.

The communication can be described in terms of its content, its form and its use. It is also important to try to distinguish between what the child can understand and how this is indicated, and what the child can express. Example: If an adult says 'Where's your coat?' it will be important to distinguish whether the child points to the coat hooks, showing understanding, or says 'Over there', speaking, pointing and looking at the same time.

Content

What sort of ideas can the child understand and/or express? What topics of conversation is the child interested in? Does the child cope equally well with all curriculum subjects? Are there words or particular ideas that the child can and cannot understand in any subjects?

Form

What form of communication does the child understand and use? For example, is it: speech; speech supplemented by gesture or exaggerated facial expression; a sign system; written language?

If the child speaks, give examples of this, written down as accurately as possible. How intelligible is the child? Does everyone understand her/him? Do other children understand her/him? Which adults understand her/him?

Indicate whether the intelligibility of the child's speech is affected by omission, substitution or distortion of words or speech sounds. Does the child have an unusual voice? Are intonation, pitch or loudness of the voice unusual? Does the child make unusual movements of the face when trying to speak?

Give examples of the language structure used and understood. Give examples of the utterances the child can understand and use.

Use

How does the child use its communication skills? Does he or she talk to everyone? Does he or she talk only to certain adults? Does he or she talk to other children? In a group? Individually? Does the child communicate: to tell news; to draw people's attention to interesting events or objects?

Try to summarise by saying how effectively the child communicates overall. Indicate areas where you feel further, more detailed assessment might be helpful and where the child might need specific help.

Tape recordings can be helpful in making a close examination of spoken language. Remember, however, that accurate transcription from a recording takes time and practice. It may take several playings to listen and write down exactly what is said, although it is usually a worthwhile exercise.

Analysis of adult-child conversation

A tape recorder can be useful for analysing how adults speak to children. The following activity often proves to be salutary, although it may also be uncomfortable at first.

Tape-record yourself talking to a child or to a group of children over a period of about five minutes. Listen to the recording and then write down your first impressions.

Listen again. Who speaks most?

You may like to have pencil and paper handy to jot down responses as you think about the following questions:

● *How many questions did you ask?*
Were they 'closed' or 'open' questions or did they ask a 'forced alternative'? Closed questions usually have only a brief factual answer, for example 'What's that?' Open questions offer an opportunity for the respondent to say more, for example, 'How are we going to find out if this ball sinks or floats?' A forced alternative such as 'Is it a cow or a horse?' can sometimes be an intermediate between the right answer required for a closed question and the completely unknown and unpredictable response to an open question. Adults are sometimes accused of playing a game of 'think what's in my head' with children – they ask a question to which they know the answer and to which only one answer will do. It is also not uncommon to see adults who sit with children looking at books and pictures saying 'What's that?', 'What's she doing?' Children may not respond as they know that the adult already knows what 'it' is and anyway they can see because the book is in front of both of

them. An element of surprise or the unknown is more likely to elicit a response. Try asking the child to draw and pass them a broken pencil, ask them to get a sweet out of a jar with a very tight lid. They may say something.

● *How long were the pauses after you spoke?*
Did they give plenty of time for a child to gather their thoughts and make a response? One teacher recently said 'I have to go quickly as we only have a twenty minute session'. That may be true but who, in that session, gets the most talking practice?

● *How many times did you start to say something and not complete it?*
Although this is very common in conversation, there is a case for saying that with children, we should make our utterances as clear and complete as possible to avoid confusion.

● *Finally, what would you change if you were to undertake these activities again?*
Most people dislike hearing themselves on tape, but there is no doubt that there is a lot to be learned from the exercise. Adults can provide children with rich opportunities to develop their speech and language. However, children who experience difficulties with language processing may be disadvantaged if the adult speaks too much or too rapidly, leaves sentences unfinished or places heavy demands on the child by asking too many questions too quickly. Adults who are aware of their own communication skills can ensure that they are helpful to children who are less skilled.

Planning what to do

Activities such as the observation of a child's communication or the tape-recording activity above provide a mass of information. The option is to take it or leave it. If it is left, there is really little value in spending time on the activity in the first place. The alternative is to examine the information carefully and think what to do next. Reflecting takes time, a rare commodity for most practitioners. However, it can be well worth taking time to think about information gathered as it can generate ideas about what to do next and therefore lead to more effective action.

The notion of 'practitioners as researchers' was introduced at the beginning of this chapter and the ideas discussed so far might well form the basis of a piece of investigation in a classroom.

For example, from language samples taken from a child in the observation exercise, a teacher may discover that a particular pupil never seems to add the final consonants to words. The next action might be to determine whether the child can hear these sounds and so the teacher devises a listening game in which children are asked to point, when the teacher calls them out, to pictures or words which sound rather similar, except for one sound, for example *car* and *cart*, *sea* and *seat*, *pie* and *pipe*. If the child in question cannot do this, but all of the other children can, then the teacher will want to look further. The teacher may decide to give the child more practice at this type of activity to see if the child's ability to hear the differences improves. If it does, then the piece of investigation has been fruitful. If the child's ability does not seem to improve, the activity has still been useful because it suggests that there may be another reason for the difficulty. The teacher will need to try something else. Perhaps the child should be referred for a hearing test, or perhaps the teacher needs to check in more detail exactly how much the child understands.

A second example of this type of reflective practice may come from the tape-recording activity. The teacher may find from the recording that certain children never seem to respond to questions. The teacher will want to consider whether the question-types might be changed, whether pauses for responses could be lengthened, or whether other children always 'jump in first' and might, perhaps temporarily, be put in a different group. Each of these possibilities can be systematically investigated to see whether they seem to make any difference.

Curriculum planning

Most teachers go through a similar cycle of planning, doing and reflecting in their development of a curriculum of suitable teaching and learning activities for their pupils. It is possible to link this with considerations about language and to cater better for the needs of pupils who have difficulties in developing speech or language. The development of suitable teaching and learning activities must be based on a staged process and must always be open to change in the light of experience and new information. Below is a framework for planning the curriculum for all children which also gives special consideration to their language needs.

A curriculum planning activity

In planning curriculum activities for a single child or a group of children, it will be helpful to consider the following:

- Long-term aims
- Short-term aims and objectives for the particular session or sessions.
- The content of the session. How will it make explicit the aims and objectives of the teaching?
- How far will the pupils be involved in, and/or made aware of the intended learning outcomes?
- How will activities incorporate the overall spoken and written (if appropriate) language abilities and needs of either the whole group of pupils or those of one or two individual pupils?
- How will human and other resources be used to support the pupils in their learning? If you are working in a team, other members of the team, speech-language therapists, classroom assistants and other teachers should be explicitly involved in the whole process.
- How will the curriculum be made suitable to meet the needs of all pupils? Review the plans by trying to evaluate them in an objective way, discussing them with the colleagues involved.

Now, you should undertake some activities based on the plans and make written notes on the outcomes. Read through the notes. Is there anything you would now change?

You should now undertake some more activities with the same pupils. Collect evidence of the pupils' learning and record this, including some examples of language used. Evaluate the activities and decide what you would do next.

In evaluating the whole cycle consider what worked and what needs changing. Consider the breadth and balance of curriculum, the choice of activities, the involvement of other adults and pupils. Consider the use of your own language; the use of resources; the classroom organisation; how tasks were presented and how pupils responded. Consider your assessment and record keeping – would it enable someone else to pick up where you had left off?

The above may seem a lengthy and tedious process but as with any complex and skilled activity, curriculum planning can become easier if it is based on a sound framework and if we are prepared to practise and to be self-critical.

Example 1: An art lesson

One teacher who undertook the activity used an art lesson incorporating a multi-sensory approach with seven children between four and six years. Each child was described as having 'very individual and specific speech and language problems'.

Additionally, 'one child, B (aged 6.3 years), stood out as particularly needing attention in areas of development involving both gross and fine motor skills. He displayed the greatest immaturity in the level of control, fluency, consistency of direction and coordination. Visual and perceptual skills appeared to be underdeveloped. During PE, in attempting to catch a ball, he was observed to turn away as the ball approached; movement was noted to lack fluency. In movement lessons, he looked down at his feet, unable to hold his head steady when standing on one leg.

When drawing, the boy used short, jerky movements, failing to look properly at the lines drawn.

In writing he had a weak pencil grip with the wrist held high rather than used for stabilisation.

In all activities, immature attention control contributed to his failure to attain a higher level of achievement. In sharing, he was described as generally uncooperative and egocentric.

The teacher concluded these observations by saying that in considering the boy's particular needs, it was necessary to set them in the context of class, group and individual lessons in order to produce a realistic and feasible plan which could encompass other children, whose needs were of equal importance. *'There is obviously a lot more teaching to do before children such as B will be in a position to benefit from a broad and balanced curriculum and before he is able to internalise and adapt experiences.'*

In her lesson plan, the teacher set up activities with the following aims:

1. to help develop perception of movement; expressing movement through line;
2. to develop manipulation skills;
3. to develop hand-eye coordination;
4. to aid early handwriting skills;
5. to explore three-dimensional and two-dimensional representation;
6. to develop attention control;
7. to encourage cooperation and partnership skills;
8. to introduce ordering and sequencing in simple patterns;
9. to encourage verbal evaluation;
10. to include the language of opposites and to develop language associated with spatial awareness.

The learning context was to be a whole-class activity leading to small group work with the help of a learning support assistant.

Activities were to include bouncing and rolling balls, following their direction. Children were to walk, then to draw the path of the ball, using thick and thin felt tip pens.

The teacher recorded on video herself and the children in the session. She then asked her colleagues to watch and comment on the recording. Below are some of the observations made on the video, by the teacher's colleagues:

1. Insufficient time was allowed for positioning of furniture so that there was inadequate space for walking activities. Although the children achieved the task, it would have been easier with more space.
2. The learning support assistant, a volunteer, did not appear to give adequate help. The children may have had better opportunity to be more vocal, demonstrating ability to use and show understanding of words if the assistant had been more fully briefed.
3. The teacher's language was inconsistent at times – for example, *fat* was intermittently replaced by *thick*; *wiggly* was replaced by *wobbly*.
4. A wide vocabulary was used. Linguistic objectives were met but opportunities should be given for children to demonstrate comprehension of vocabulary in other ways and in other contexts.
5. Group cooperation was good. Turn-taking was appropriate.
6. Attention was maintained throughout the session. Even B, despte a brief spell of inactivity, was brought back to task each time.
7. Observation and evaluation by the children was limited by teacher-led statements and questions. Opportunities to let the children talk more freely should be offered in future lessons.
8. Cognitive objectives were met; there was repetition of actions leading to hand-eye coordination, two-dimensional representation of physical movement resulting in practice of manipulation skills.
9. The lesson digressed in order to develop a child's observation arising from experimentation: it was discovered that a fat pen, when angled, could produce a thin line. 'I made thin one' was the excited message conveyed. Sequencing of fat and thin lines to create patterns followed.

The lesson was judged successful in many areas. The observations and comments of supportive colleagues however, gave suggestions for ways to develop and improve it further.

The teacher summarised by saying that one main strategy which would be retained was the planning of short, achievable activities which related to those in the first lesson but differed sufficiently to extend interest and experience. Now that the children had used movement to define pattern and represent line, it would be important to see if they could transfer the vocabulary and concepts to other situations. The teacher planned that the next lesson would retain the main aims and objectives but that the language aims would be narrowed by focusing on one main activity. The children would be given more opportunity to 'discuss', prompted by the teacher's language, which would incorporate question forms. Repetition of aspects of the first lesson would allow the children to recall and repeat prior experiences before moving on to this next lesson.

Example 2: Mathematics in a primary class

In the next example, a teacher used this reflective approach in the teaching of mathematics to a group of primary school children with language difficulties. She had attempted to use published mathematics worksheets with the children. However, as she observed, 'The very fact that most schemes are introduced with the explicit aim of using language to help learning does not help the child with language difficulties.' Her class had problems with the written instructions in maths worksheets. She noted that workbooks used a very wide variety of language for the same mathematical operation and seemed to jump from one concept to another as the child progressed through the book. Even more problems arose when the language became more abstract, which happened quite early in the scheme.

A considerable amount of adaptation of the materials was needed and children required a great deal of teacher support as each new mathematical operation was introduced. The teacher said she knew that even with careful planning and repeated explanations, children often operated mechanically, without understanding, and were often unable to transfer their skills to new situations. The scheme's assessment procedure did not help in planning for individuals as, although it noted that the children were failing in certain areas, it did not identify why and what the next step should be.

Children with language difficulties may experience particular problems in understanding number as they may have:

1. a weakness in symbolic understanding;
2. a weakness in organisation of thought and experience;
3. a memory weakness;
4. a lack of vocabulary and concepts relevant to early number work;
5. a weakness in auditory discrimination and, for some children;
6. an almost total reliance on sign language.

(Grauberg 1985)

The teacher therefore would need to consider the essential skills the children already had and would need to consider carefully any language component of mathematical tasks. She decided to assess the children's skills using first the Mathematics Assessment Procedure, 'MAP' (Donlan and Hutt 1990) and the Primary Language Record (Barrs et al. 1990). Additionally, each child was videoed attempting to complete a 'missing number' task (For example 3+?= 5).

Her notes on one child, 'R', are summarised below.

R was unable to complete the 'missing number' task successfully by 'counting on' to the answer. He also failed to see the relationship between addition and subtraction and that either of these operations could be used in the missing number task.

The assessment using the MAP procedure highlighted certain weaknesses, the most surprising of which was R's inability to understand one-to-one correspondence. The assessment also pinpointed difficulties with 'sentences and symbols' tasks, which indicated a weakness in understanding the mathematical symbols involved.

The first stage of the teaching sessions had to be to break down the task involved and to carefully monitor the child's understanding of each stage before planning for the next step.

In the first session the teacher planned a more practical approach, rather than the workbook focus she had previously used. She would use sweets and a tin with magnetic numbers and plus and minus symbols. For example, she would put one sweet in the tin, put the number 1 on the lid and ask 'How many?' Then she would add a sweet, put '+1' on the lid and ask 'How many now?' When the child gave the correct answer, the magnetic symbols '= 2' were put on the lid.

Additionally the boy was given 'number sentences' ('Two plus three equals?') to complete and was given a calculator to check results.

The speech and language therapist would be involved in developing vocabulary associated with these activities both inside the classroom with the teacher and outside the classroom in order to generalise the work to other situations.

Observation during the lesson suggested that R became more aware of symbols and their meaning. However, he was still confused about the order of symbols used in number sentences. The video of the session showed that R's concentration on the task was limited, something the teacher had previously been unaware of. At one point the teacher thought that R was looking at the task when he was, in fact, looking across the room.

When working independently, he would complete a small part of a task and then stop until encouraged to carry on.

A number of specific problems were identified in R's mathematical learning:

Problem 1: Sequencing things from left to right as when required to write down number sentences. Organisation of himself and his materials was noted to be poor at various parts of his school day.

Future work: would need to focus on rhythm and sequencing, in PE, using the computer and with the speech and language therapist. An arrow from left to right was taped to his table as a visual reminder to R of the sequence of learning at all times. In PE he should be encouraged to organise himself and his clothes before and after the lesson. He should also be encouraged to ask if he is unsure of what to do next – he had been observed standing with book and pencil at his table for some time as there seemed to be no obvious place for him to sit. His confidence needed to be built.

Problem 2: R appeared to forget where he was in the sequence of work, his teacher's instructions and the numbers he was working with. Short-term memory would need further investigation

Action: Work with the speech-language therapist and the teacher to examine this and work on it further.

Problem 3: Poor number formation and fine motor skills generally slowed his work down.

Future work: General activities to develop motor skills including use of pencil grip, pencil control work, cutting and construction skills during art and technology.

Problem 4: Poor task concentration. Unable to reflect on and extend his learning.

Action: Activities to develop functional communication in the classroom. Link this with National Curriculum speaking and listening attainment targets.

The teacher summarised her reflections on the 'future implications for the teaching of mathematics in my classroom':

> 'By focusing on one particular child's problems in coping with the mathematical operation of missing numbers, I have learned a great deal. This will have obvious implications, not only for that child's individual programme but for my whole approach to planning and organisation in this area of the curriculum.' She continued:

1. Initial and careful individual assessment should highlight any areas for concern in a child's basic mathematical thinking and language.
2. Monitoring progress. The video was extremely useful in pinpointing problems of which I was previously unaware and made me think about things I had taken for granted about a child's mathematical learning. The Primary Language Record's sheet provided a useful framework for my observations. Keeping this structure in mind, I have developed a simpler observation sheet (Figure 10.1). The basic format can be used for other areas of the curriculum and useful evidence of a child's language and learning across the curriculum could be collected.
3. The importance of teamwork. The advice and support of other professionals is essential if an individual programme which looks at the whole child, rather than just areas of the curriculum, is to be established.
4. The need to move away from one mathematics scheme and use National Curriculum programmes of study as a guide or framework for learning. This will require a great deal of time and effort on behalf of all staff concerned.

Example 3

This example shows how improved collaboration between professionals was of benefit in curriculum planning for an eight-year-old girl, S, in a mainstream class, who was reported to have difficulties at the semantic and pragmatic levels of language.

By tape-recording a lesson, the teacher was able to note that S had not seemed to understand concepts of 'enough', 'not enough' and 'too much'.

In discussion with the speech and language therapist, the teacher decided to note areas of the curriculum where the lack of use of these terms could be a problem. Use of money seemed to be the most obvious. Although S could make up amounts of money to 50p, could subtract number to 20 and had plenty of experience of going shopping and role playing in the class shop she did not seem to grasp the concept of change. She was observed in a situation with two other children in the shop and while they made comments such as 'You've given me too much. There's your change', S's comments tended to be, 'That's correct' or 'That's wrong'. This suggested that a curriculum target was possibly being hindered by an aspect of the girl's language difficulties.

Aims and activities were planned to develop S's understanding and use of the terms 'enough', 'not enough' and 'too much' in practical situations. Other teachers and S's parents were informed about this and were asked to exaggerate their use of this language to engage S's attention in a variety of language contexts.

It became clear early on that S had a good understanding of the concepts 'enough', 'not enough' and 'too much' in natural and spontaneously arising situations and she demonstrated this by completing worksheets. However, when change was introduced in shopping activities, S demonstrated confusion even though the teacher used a number of different approaches.

Because S enjoyed role play, it was decided to give her a set 'script' to use – 'That's too much; I have to give you change'. She quickly adopted this although she still required considerable concrete help to work things out. 'Over-teaching' was continued until S was becoming quicker at working through the process and could eventually complete written worksheets. After three weeks S reached her target and by appearing to inwardly rehearse the set dialogue, she seemed to have a strategy which helped her. Her parents reported that she could now go to the local shop to spend her pocket money.

This process continued until S was competent to use 20p. She had then successfully completed Level A in mathematics – Money target (Scottish curriculum).

The teacher's reflections note: 'It is not our normal practice to set down a target which on the surface appears to be many steps from the starting point but it helped us to think a process through in a structured way and be aware of how the assistance of a variety of people could be utilised. It required a lot of consultation and liaison with the speech and language therapist who

\begin{tabular}{c} \textbf{Mathematics} \end{tabular}				

Mathematics

Name _____   Key Stage _____

Date _____   Att. _____

Date	Activity	Related language	Level	Comments

Language Across the Curriculum

Figure 10.1

normally worked with S on a "withdrawal basis". She commented on how much she had enjoyed being part of the process from the beginning to end and both the class teacher and myself also felt that this had been a success as pedagogical decisions were shared by all of us and monitored and adapted where necessary along the way.

Having now focused so closely on the curriculum planning, teaching and assessment we have already been forced to review a more satisfactory method of recording cross-curricular activities which may involve other disciplines in the learning and teaching of a child with language difficulties in a mainstream classroom.'

The examples above are very different from each other. It may be difficult to imagine how they could help in finding solutions to work with other young people with language difficulties. A teacher who undertook the task reported: 'It was an extremely valuable exercise in that we have now absorbed all those laborious steps into mental activity. The exercise can now be used for (other) subjects . . . It is just not possible in mainstream to keep such detailed records. However, it was . . . most beneficial . . . as far as my own teaching style was concerned.'

If we try to understand the principles the teachers were using, then they may be applicable to other, very individual cases.

First, it is important to note that the teachers took a very close look at the children and the strengths and weaknesses of their language for the intended learning. They also looked at themselves, as managers of the children's learning. Although, in two of the examples, the teachers based their curriculum work on available schemes or programmes, a considerable amount of adaptation was necessary to make them useful to an individual child. Each teacher undertook very careful matching of the child's language and other skills with the curriculum materials and their own language of instruction. In each case, too, the teacher enlisted the help of colleagues, either to help with the planning, to observe and comment on the lesson or to undertake specific parts of the teaching. Each teacher was prepared to examine closely what they were doing, to evaluate it and, where necessary, to rethink and change their plans. Such activities are not easy and are always time-consuming. However, they can lead to more effective teaching and can lead to less frustrating experiences for teachers and pupils alike.

Conclusion

It is appropriate to conclude this book with a chapter based on classroom practice. All practitioners want to know how colleagues approach their work. Teachers who write up these sorts of activities for others to read can provide extremely valuable information. Where children are considered to have special educational needs, it may be particularly useful to see whether any of the ideas described could transfer to other contexts.

Further reading

Martin, D. and Miller, C. (1999) *Language and the Curriculum: Practitioner Research in Planning Differentiation*. London: David Fulton Publishers.
Ripley, K., Barrett, J. and Fleming, P. (2001) *Inclusion for Children with Speech and Language Impairments*. London: David Fulton Publishers.

References

Adams, C. (2001) 'Clinical diagnostic and intervention studies of children with semantic-pragmatic language disorder', *International Journal of Language and Communication Disorders*, 36(3): 289–305.

Adams, C., Byers Brown, B. and Edwards, M. (1997) *Developmental Disorders of Language*, (2nd edn). London: Whurr.

Adams, C., Nightingale, C., Hesketh, A. and Hall, R. (2000) 'Targeting metaphonological ability in intervention for children with developmental phonological disorders', *Child Language Teaching and Therapy*, 16(3): 285–99.

Adult Literacy and Basic Skills Unit (1988) *After the Act: Developing Basic Skills Work in the 1990s*. London: Adult Literacy and Basic Skills Unit.

AFASIC (1991) *AFASIC Checklists*. Wisbech: Language Development Aids.

AFASIC (1993) *Alone and Anxious: Parents' Experience of the Services Offered to Children with Speech and Language Impairments*. London: AFASIC.

Aitchison, J. (1994) *Words in the Mind*. Oxford: Blackwell.

Aitchison, J. (1999) *Linguistics: An Introduction*. London: Hodder and Stoughton.

Anderson-Wood, L. and Smith, B.R. (1997) *Working with Pragmatics*. Bicester: Winslow.

Anthony, A., Bogle, D., Ingram, T.T.S. and McIsaac, M.W. (1971) *The Edinburgh Articulation Test*. Edinburgh: Livingstone.

Bamford, J. and Saunders, E. (1985) *Hearing Impairment, Auditory Imperception and Language Disability*. London: Whurr.

Barrs, M., Ellis, S., Hester, H. and Thomas, A. (1990) *Patterns of Learning: The Primary Language Record and the National Curriculum*. London: Centre for Language in Primary Education.

Beard, R. and Oakhill, J. (1994) *Reading by Apprenticeship?* Slough: NFER-Nelson.

Bishop, D.M.V. (1983) *Test for Reception of Grammar (TROG)*. Available from Dept of Psychology, University of Manchester, UK.

Bishop, D.M.V. (1998) 'Development of the Children's Communication Checklist (CCC): a method for assessing qualitative aspects of communicative impairment', *Journal of Child Psychology and Psychiatry*, 39, 879–93.

Bishop, D.M.V. (2000) 'Pragmatic language impairment : a correlate of SLI, a distinct subgroup or part of the autistic continuum?' in D.V.M. Bishop and L.B. Leonard (eds) *Speech and Language Impairments: Causes, Characteristics, Intervention and Outcome*. Hove: Psychology Press, pp.99–114.

Bishop, D.M.V. and Adams, C. (1989) 'Conversational characteristics of children with semantic-pragmatic disorders. II: What features lead to a judgement of inappropriacy?', *British Journal of Disorders of Communication*, 24, 241–61.

Bloom, L. (1973) *One Word at a Time: The Use of Single-word Utterances before Syntax*. The Hague: Mouton.

Bloom, L. and Lahey, M. (1978) *Language Development and Language Disorders*. New York: Wiley.

Boucher, J. (1998) 'SPD as a distinct diagnostic entity: logical considerations and direction for future research', *International Journal of Language and Communication Disorders*, 33, 71–81.

Bower, T. (1977) *The Perceptual World of the Child*. Glasgow: Fontana/Open Books.

Bowerman, M. (1980) 'The structure and origin of semantic categories in the language of the learning child', in D. Foster and S. Brandes (eds) *Symbol as Sense. New Approaches to the Analysis of Meaning*. New York: Academic Press.

Bradley, L. and Bryant, P. E. (1983) 'Categorising sounds and learning to read: a causal connection', *Nature* 301, 419–21.

Bradley, L. and Bryant, P. E. (1985) *Rhyme and Reason in Reading and Spelling*. Ann Arbor, Mi: University of Michigan Press.

Brown, R. (1973) *A First Language: The Early Stages*. Cambridge, Ma: Harvard University Press.

Browne, A. (2001) *Developing Language and Literacy 3–8*. London: Paul Chapman. 2nd edn.

Bruner, J. (1986) *Actual Minds, Possible Worlds*. Cambridge, Ma: Harvard University Press.

Chall, J. (1983) *Stages in Reading Development*. New York: McGraw-Hill.

Child, E. (1982) 'Individual and social factors associated with behaviour of children in a play setting', unpublished PhD thesis, Aston University, Birmingham, UK.

Chomsky, C. (1969) *The Acquisition of Syntax in Children from 5 to 10*. Cambridge, Ma: MIT Press.

Chomsky, N. (1959) 'Review of *Verbal Behaviour* by B.F. Skinner', *Language*, 35, 26–58.

Cline, T. and Shamsi, T. (2000) *Language Needs or Special Needs? The assessment of Learning Difficulties in Literacy among Children Learning English as an Additional Language: A Literature Review*. London: DfEE Publications.

Cobuild English Language Dictionary (1987). London: Collins.

Conti-Ramsden, G. and Botting, N. (1999) 'Characteristics of children attending language units in England: a national study of 7-year-olds', *International Journal of Language and Communication Disorders*, 34(4): 359–66.

Conti-Ramsden, G., Botting, N., Simkin, Z. (2001) 'Follow-up of children attending infant language units: outcomes at 11 years of age.' *International Journal of Language and Communication Disorders*, 36(2): 207–19.

Cooke, A. (2001) 'Critical response to: "Dyslexia, Literacy and Psychological Assessment" (Report by a Working Party of the Division of Educational and Child Psychology of the British Psychology Society)', *Dyslexia*, 7, 47–52.

Cooke, A. (2002) 'Case study: a virtual non-reader achieves a degree', *Dyslexia*, 8(2): 102–115.

Cooper, J., Moodley, M. and Reynell, I. (1978) *Helping Language Development*. London: Edward Arnold.

Cromer, R.F. (1991) *Language and Thought in Normal and Handicapped Children*. Oxford: Blackwell.

Crystal, D. (1981) *Clinical Linguistics*. Wein: Springer-Verlag.

Crystal, D. (1983) *Profiling Linguistic Disability*. London: Edward Arnold.

Crystal, D. (1987) 'Teaching vocabulary: the case for a semantic curriculum'. *Child Language Teaching and Therapy*, 3, 40–56.

Crystal, D., Fletcher, P. and Garman, M. (1976) *Grammatical Analysis of Language Disability*. London: Edward Arnold.

Crystal, D. and Varley, R. (1998) *An Introduction to Language Pathology*. London: Whurr. 4th edn.

Dahl, R. (1988) *Matilda.* Harmondsworth: Penguin.

Dalton, P. and Hardcastle, W. (1989) *Disorders of Fluency.* London: Whurr. 2nd edn.

Daniels, H. and Anghileri, J. (1995) *Secondary Mathematics and Special Educational Needs.* London: Cassell.

Dean, E., Howell, J., Hill, A. and Waters, D. (1990) *Metaphon Resource Pack.* Windsor: NFER-Nelson.

Department for Education (1994) *Code of Practice on the Identification and Assessment of Special Educational Needs.* London: Department for Education/Welsh Office.

Department for Education and Employment and Qualifications and Curriculum Authority (1999) *The National Curriculum: Handbook for Teachers in England Key Stages 1 and 2.* London: DfEE and QCA.

Department for Education and Employment (1998a) *Special Educational Needs: a Programme of Action.* London: Department for Education and Employment.

Department for Education and Employment (1998b) *The National Literacy Strategy: Framework for Teaching.* London: DfEE.

Department for Education and Employment and Department of Health (2000) *Speech and Language Therapy Services to Children (England).* London: DfEE/DH.

Department for Education and Skills (2001) *Special Educational Needs Code of Practice.* London: Department for Education and Skills.

DES (1989) *Report of the English Working Party 5–16 (the Cox Report).* London: HMSO.

de Villiers, L.G. and de Villiers, P.A. (1973) 'A cross-sectional study of the acquisition of grammatical morphemes in child speech', *Journal of Psycholinguistic Research,* 2, 67–78.

Dewart, H. and Summers, S. (1995) *The Pragmatics Profile of Everyday Communication Skills in Children.* Windsor: NFER-Nelson.

Disability Rights Commission (2001) *Draft Code of Practice (schools).* London: Disability Rights Commission

Dockrell, J. and Lindsay, G. (1998) 'The ways in which speech and language difficulties impact on children's access to the curriculum', *Child Language Teaching and Therapy,* 14(2): 117–33.

Dockrell, J. and McShane, J. (1993) *Children's Learning Difficulties: A Cognitive Approach.* Oxford: Blackwell.

Dockrell, J., Messer, D., George, R. and Wilson, G. (1998) 'Children with word-finding difficulties – prevalence, presentation and naming problems', *International Journal of Language and Communication Disorders,* 33(4): 445–54.

Dockrell, J. and Messer, D. (1999) *Children's Language and Communication Difficulties.* London: Cassell.

Dollaghan, C. (1987) 'Comprehension monitoring in normal and language impaired children', *Topics in Language Disorders,* 7, 45–60.

Donaldson, M. (1978) *Children's Minds.* Glasgow: Fontana/Collins.

Donlan, C. and Hutt, E. (1990) *Mathematics Assessment Procedure for Young Language Impaired Children.* London: I CAN.

Donlan, C. and Masters, J. (2000) 'Correlates of social development in children with communicative disorders: the concurrent predictive value of verbal short-term memory span', *International Journal of Language and Communication Disorders,* 35(2): 211–26.

Doyle, R. (1993) *Paddy Clarke ha ha ha.* London: Minerva.

Dulay, H. and Burt, M. (1977) 'Some remarks on creativity in second language acquisition', in M.Burt, H. Dulay, and M. Finnochiaro (eds) *Viewpoints on English as a Second Language.* New York: Regent Press.

Duncan, D. (ed.) (1989) *Working with Bilingual Language Disability*. London: Chapman and Hall.

Dunn, L.M., Whetton, C. and Pintilie, D. (1982) *British Picture Vocabulary Scales*. Windsor: NFER-Nelson.

Durgunoglu, A., Nagy, W.E. and Hancin-Bhatt, B. J. (1993) 'Cross-language transfer of phonological awareness', *Journal of Educational Psychology*, 85(3): 453–65.

Edwards, S., Fletcher, P., Garman, M., Hughes, A., Letts, C. and Sinka, I. (1997) *Reynell Developmental Language Scales (RDLS III)*. Windsor: NFER-Nelson.

Edwards, V. (1995) *Reading in Multilingual Classrooms*. Reading and Language Information Centre: University of Reading.

Elliott, C. (1996) *British Abilities Scale* 2nd edn. Windsor: NFER-Nelson.

Evans, J.L. (2002) 'Variability in comprehension strategy use in children with SLI: a dynamic systems account', *International Journal of Language and Communication Disorders,* 37(2): 95–131.

Fantini, A.E. (1985) *Language Acquisition of a Bilingual Child: A Sociolinguistic Perspective*. Avon: Multilingual Matters.

Fathman, A. (1975) 'The relationship between first and second language productive ability', *Language Learning*, 25(2): 245–53.

Foster, S.H. (1990) *The Communicative Competence of Young Children*. New York: Longman.

Fowler, W. (1962) 'Teaching a two-year-old to read: an experiment in early childhood learning', *Genetic Psychology Monographs*, 66, 181–283.

Galton, M. and Willocks, J. (eds) (1983) *Moving from the Primary Classroom*. London: Routledge and Kegan Paul.

Garcia, J. (2001) President's message, *NABE* 25, 2, Nov/Dec 2001, p.1.

German, D. J. (1986) National College of Education *Test of Word Finding (TWF)*. Allen, Texas: DLM Teaching Resources.

Giles, H. and Powesland, P.F. (1978) *Speech Style and Social Evaluation*. London: Academic Press.

Goswami. U. (1988) 'Children's use of analogy in learning to spell', *British Journal of Developmental Psychology*, 6, 21–33.

Goswami, U. (1992) 'Annotation: Phonological factors in spelling development', *Journal of Child Psychology and Psychiatry*, 33(6): 967–75.

Goswami, U. and Bryant, P. (1990) *Phonological Skills and Learning to Read*. Hove: Lawrence Erlbaum.

Grauberg, E. (1985) 'Some problems in the early stages of teaching numbers to language handicapped children'. *Child Language Teaching and Therapy*, 1(1): 17–29.

Grunwell, P. (1987) *Clinical Phonology*. 2nd edn. London: Croom Helm.

Halliday, M.A.K. (1973) *Learning How to Mean: Explorations in the Development of Language*. London: Edward Arnold.

Halliday, M.A.K. and Hasan, R. (1976) *Cohesion in English*. London: Longman.

Hardman, F. and Beverton, S. (1993) 'Cooperative group work and the development of metadiscoursal skills', *Support for Learning*, 8(4): 146–50.

Harris, J. (1990) *Early Language Development: Implications for Clinical and Educational Practice*. London: Routledge.

Harris, M. and Coltheart, M. (1986) *Language Processing in Children and Adults: An Introduction*. London: Routledge and Kegan Paul.

Henderson, E. (1985) *Teaching Spelling*. Boston: Houghton Mifflin.

Hesketh, A., Adams, C., Nightingale, C. and Hall, R. (2000) 'Phonological awareness therapy and articulatory training approaches for children with phonological disorders: a comparative outcome study', *International Journal of Language and*

Communication Disorders, 35(3): 337–54.

Holm, A. and Dodd, B. (1999) 'An intervention case study of a bilingual child with phonological disorder', *Child Language Teaching and Therapy,* 15(2): 139–58.

Howell, J. and Dean, E. (1994) *Treating Phonological Disorders in Children: Metaphon – Theory to Practice.* London: Whurr.

Howlin, P. and Cross, P. (1994) 'The variability of language test scores in 3- and 4- year olds children of normal non-verbal intelligence: a brief research report', *European Journal of Disorders of Communication,* 29: 279–88.

Humphrey, N. (2002) 'Teacher and pupil ratings of self-esteem in developmental dyslexia', *British Journal of Special Education* 29(1): 29–36.

I CAN (2001) *Joint Professional Development Framework.* London: I CAN.

Ingram, D. (1989) *Phonological Disability in Children.* 2nd edn. London: Whurr.

Jefferies, E. and Dolan, S. (1994) 'Reluctant talkers in the early years: some key issues', in J. Watson (ed.) *Working with Communication Difficulties.* Edinburgh: Moray House Publications.

Knowles, W. and Masidlover. M. (1982) *Derbyshire Language Scheme.* Derbyshire County Council, Ripley, Derbyshire, UK.

Knowles, W. and Masidlover, M. (1987) *Derbyshire Rapid Screening Test.* Educational Psychology Service, Derbyshire County Council, Ripley, Derbyshire, UK.

Ladefoged. P. (1982) *A Course in Phonetics.* 2nd edn. New York: Harcourt Brace Jovanovich Inc.

Lacey, P. (2001) *Support Partnerships: Collaboration in Action.* London: David Fulton Publishers.

Lahey, M. (1988) *Language Disorders and Language Development.* New York: Macmillan.

Landells, J. (1989) 'Assessment of semantics', in K. Grundy (ed.) *Linguistics in Clinical Practice.* London: Whurr.

Law, J., Lindsay, G., Peacey, N., Gascoigne, M., Soloff, N., Radford, J. Band, S. with Fitzgerald, L. (2000) *Provision for Children with Speech and Language Needs in England and Wales: Facilitating Communication between Education and Health Services.* London: Department for Education and Employment Research Report RR239.

Layton, L. and Deeny, K. (1995) 'Tackling literacy difficulties: can teacher training meet the challenge?', *British Journal of Special Education,* 22(1): 20–3.

Lee, L. (1971) *Northwestern Syntax Screening Test.* Northwestern University Press.

Leinonen, E. and Letts, C. (1997) 'Referential communication tasks: performance by normal and pragmatically impaired children', *European Journal of Disorders of Communication* 32: 53–65.

Lenneberg, E. (1967) *The Biological Foundations of Language.* New York: Wiley.

Lewis, A. (1990) 'Six and seven year old normal children's talk to peers with severe learning difficulties'. *European Journal of Special Needs Education* 5(1): 13–23.

Lindsay, G. and Dockrell, J. (2000) 'The behaviour and self-esteem of children with specific speech and language difficulties', *British Journal of Educational Psychology,* 70: 583–601.

Locke, A. and Beech, M. (1991) *Teaching Talking.* Windsor: NFER-Nelson.

Locke, A., Ginsborg, J. and Peers, I. (2002) 'Development and disadvantage: implications for the early years and beyond', *International Journal of Language and Communication Disorders* 37(1): 3–15.

Mackay, D., Thompson, B. and Schaub, P. (1979) *Breakthrough to Literacy: Teacher's Manual.* 2nd edition. London: Longmans for the Schools Council.

Macnamara, J. (1982) *Names for Things.* Cambridge, Ma.: MIT Press.

McCartney, E. (ed.) (1999) *Speech/language Therapists and Teachers Working Together: A Systems Approach to Collaboration.* London: Whurr.

McTear, M. (1985) 'Pragmatic disorder: a case study of conversational disability', *British Journal of Disorders of Communication,* 20(2): 129–42.

Malmer, G. (2000) 'Mathematics and dyslexia – an overlooked connection', *Dyslexia,* 6(4): 223–30.

Martin, D., Miller, C., Perks, P. and Prestage, S. (1992) *Taping the Key Stage 3 Pilot Mathematics Tests.* Report to the Schools Examination and Assessment Council, School of Education, University of Birmingham.

Martin, D. and Reilly, O. (1995) 'Global language delay: analysis of a severe central auditory processing deficit', in M. Perkins and S. Howard (eds) *Case Studies in Clinical Linguistics.* London: Whurr.

Miles, E. (1989) *The Bangor Dyslexia Teaching System.* London: Whurr.

Miller, C. (1999) 'Teachers and speech and language therapists, a shared framework', *British Journal of Special Education,* 26(3): 141–46.

Nelson, K. (1981) 'Individual differences in language development: implications for development and language', *Developmental Psychology,* 17, 170–87.

Newton, M.J. and Thomson, M.E. (1982) *Aston Index (Revised).* Wisbech, Cambs: Learning Development Aids.

Nippold, M. (1999) 'Word definition in adolescents as a function of reading proficiency: a research note', *Child Language Teaching and Therapy* 15(2): 171–76.

Norwich, B. (1990) *Reappraising Special Needs Education.* London: Cassell.

Nuthall, G. and Church, J. (1973) 'Experimental studies of teaching behaviour', in G. O'Hara, M. and Johnston, J. (1997) 'Syntactic bootstrapping in children with specific language impairment', *European Journal of Disorders of Communication,* 32(2): 189–205.

Payton, P. and Winfield, M. (2000) 'Interventions for pupils with dyspraxic difficulties', *Dyslexia,* 6: 208–10.

Peer, L. and Reid, G. (eds) (2000) *Multilingualism, Literacy and Dyslexia: A Challenge for Educators.* London: David Fulton Publishers.

Pembry, M. (1992) 'Genetics and language disorder', in P. Fletcher and D. Hall (eds) *Specific Speech and Language Disorders in Children.* London: Whurr.

Perera, K. (1986) 'Language acquisition and writing', in P. Fletcher and M. Garman (eds) *Language Acquisition.* 2nd edn. Cambridge: Cambridge University Press.

Perera, K. (1992) 'Reading and writing in the National Curriculum', in P. Fletcher and D. Hall, *Specific Speech and Language Disorders in Children.* London: Whurr.

Pollock, J. (2001) 'I.Q Tests', *Dyslexia,* 7: 171–73.

Pollock, J. and Walker, E. (1994) *Day to Day Dyslexia in the Classroom.* London: Taylor Francis.

Precious, A. and Conti-Ramsden, G. (1988) 'Language impaired children's comprehension of active versus passive sentences', *The British Journal of Disorders of Communication,* 23(3): 229–43.

Pumfrey, P. (1991) *Improving Children's Reading in the Junior School: Challenges and Responses.* London: Cassell Educational Ltd.

Pumfrey, P. and Reason, R. (1991) *Specific Learning Difficulties (Dyslexia): Challenges and Responses.* London and New York: Routledge.

Rawle, Graham (1992) *More Lost Consonants.* London: Fourth Estate.

Read, C. (1986) *Children's Creative Spelling.* London: Routledge and Kegan Paul.

Renfrew, C. (1972) *The Bus Story.* Bicester: Winslow.

Richards, B. (1994) 'Child-directed speech and influences on language acquisition: methodology and interpretation', in C. Galloway and B.J. Richards (eds) *Input and*

Interaction in Language Acquisition. Cambridge: Cambridge University Press.

Richards, M. (1974) *The Integration of a Child into a Social World*. Cambridge: Cambridge University Press.

Rinaldi, W. (1992) *The Social Use of Language Programme (SULP)*. Windsor: NFER-Nelson.

Robinson, G. (1990) 'Positive and negative roles (13–15)', in A. Wilkinson, A. Davies and D. Berrill (eds) *Spoken English Illuminated*. Milton Keynes: Open University Press.

Robson, P. (1984) 'Prewalking locomotor movements and their use in predicting standing and walking', *Child Care, Health and Development*, 10, 317–30.

Royal College of Speech and Language Therapists (1996) *Communicating Quality 2: Professional Standards for Speech and Language Therapists*. London: College of Speech and Language Therapists.

Semel, E., Wiig, E. and Secord, W. (1997) *Clinical Evaluation of Language Fundamentals Test (CELF–R UK)*, revised UK edn., Hove: Psychological Corporation.

Sinclair Taylor, A. (1995) '"Less better than the rest": perceptions of integration in a multi-ethnic special needs unit', *Educational Review*, 47(3): 263–74.

Skinner, B.F. (1957) *Verbal Behaviour*. New York: Appleton-Century-Crofts.

Snowling, M. (1985) *Children's Written Language Difficulties: Assessment and Management*. Windsor: NFER-Nelson.

Snowling, M. (2001) 'From language to reading and dyslexia', *Dyslexia*, 7(1): 37–46.

Stacey, K. (1994) 'Contextual assessment of young children: moving from the strange to the familiar and from theory to praxis', *Child Language Teaching and Therapy*, 10(2): 179–98.

Stackhouse, J. (1989) 'Relationship between spoken and written language disorders', in K. Mogford and J. Sadler (eds) *Child Language Disability: Implications in an Educational Setting*. Clevedon: Multilingual Matters.

Stackhouse, J. and Wells, B. (1993) 'Psycholinguistic assessment of developmental speech disorders', *European Journal of Disorders of Communication*, 28,4: 331–48.

Stackhouse, J. and Wells, B. (1997) *Children's Speech and Literacy Difficulties: A Psycholinguistic Framework*. London: Whurr Publishing.

Stackhouse, J. and Wells, B. (eds) (2001) *Children's Speech and Literacy Difficulties: Identification and Intervention*. London: Whurr Publishing.

Stampe, D. (1972) 'Dissertation on Natural Phonology'. Unpublished PhD dissertation. University of Chicago.

Stanovich, K. (1994) 'Annotation: Does dyslexia exist?', *Journal of Child Psychology and Psychiatry*, 35(4): 579–95.

Stevenson, J., Richman, N. and Graham, P. (1985) 'Behaviour problems and language abilities at three years and behavioural deviance at eight years', *Journal of Child Psychology and Psychiatry*, 26(2): 215–30.

Teacher Training Agency (1999) *National SEN Specialist Standards*. London: Teacher Training Agency.

Thordardottir, E. and Weismer, S.E. (2001) 'High-frequency verbs and verb diversity in the spontaneous speech of school-age children with specific language impairment', *International Journal of Language and Communication Disorders*, 36(2): 221–44.

Tizard, B. and Hughes, M. (1984) *Young Children Learning: Talking and Thinking at Home and at School*. London: Fontana.

Townsend, P. and Davidson, N. (1982) *Inequalities in Health: The Black Report*. Harmondsworth: Penguin.

Treiman, R. (1993) *Beginning to Spell: a Study of First Grade Children*. Oxford: Oxford University Press.

Ukrainetz, T. and Blomquist, C. (2002) 'The criterion validity of four vocabulary tests compared with a language sample', *Child Language Teaching and Therapy*, 18(1): 59–78.

UNESCO (1994) *The UNESCO Salamanca Statement*. World Conference on Special Educational Needs, Salamanca, Spain. Paris: UNESCO.

van der Lely, H. (1994) 'Canonical linking rules: forward versus reverse linking in normally developing and specifically language impaired children', *Cognition*, 51, 29–72.

van Riper, C. and Irwin, J. (1958) *Voice and Articulation*. Englewood Cliffs, NJ: Prentice Hall.

Vygotsky, L.S. (1962) *Thought and Language*. Cambridge, Ma.: MIT Press.

Walker, M. (1978) 'The Makaton Vocabulary', in *Ways and Means* (coordinator, T. Tebbs). London: Globe Education.

Walker, M. and Armfield, A. (1981) 'What is the Makaton Vocabulary?', *Special Education:Forward Trends*, 8(3): 19–20.

Wardhaugh, R. (1985) *How Conversation Works*. Oxford: Blackwell.

Wardhaugh, R. (1995) *Understanding English Grammar: A Linguistic Approach*. Oxford: Blackwell.

Watcyn-Jones, P. and Howard-Williams, D. (2001) *Grammar Games and Activities 1*. Penguin English Photocopiables, Harlow: Pearson Education Ltd.

Watson, I. (1991) 'Phonological processing in two languages', in E. Bialystok, (ed.) *Language Processing in Bilingual Children*. Cambridge: Cambridge University Press.

Wells, G. (1985) *Language Development in the Preschool Years*. Cambridge: Cambridge University Press.

Wells, G. (1986) *The Meaning Makers: Children Learning Language and Using Language to Learn*. London: Hodder and Stoughton.

Wendon, J. (1984) *Letterland*. Cambridge: Letterland.

Wheldall, K., Mittler, P., Hobsbaum, A, Duncan, D., Gibbs, D. and Saund, S. (1987) *The Revised Sentence Comprehension Test with the Panjabi Version*. Windsor: NFER-Nelson.

White, L. (1987) 'Against comprehensible input', *Applied Linguistics*, 8(2): 95–110.

Wiig, E., Semel, E. and Nysrom, I. (1982) 'Comparison of rapid naming abilities in language-learning disabled and academically achieving eight-year-olds', *Language, Speech and Hearing Services in Schools*, 13, 11–23

Wood, D., Wood, H., Griffiths, A. and Howarth, I. (1986) *Teaching and Talking with Deaf Children*. London: John Wiley and Sons.

Wood, D. (1988) *How Children Think and Learn*. Oxford: Blackwell.

Wood, J., Wright, J. and Stackhouse, J. (2000) *Language and Literacy: joining together*. London: BDA and AFASIC

Wray, A. (2001) 'Formulaic sequences in second language teaching: principle and practice', *Applied Linguistics*, 21(4): 463–89.

Wright, J. (1992) 'Collaboration between speech and language therapists and teachers', in P. Fletcher and D. Hall (eds) *Specific Speech and Language Disorders in Children*. London: Whurr.

Author index

Subject index